Frank Leslie

Incidents of the Civil War in America

Frank Leslie

Incidents of the Civil War in America

ISBN/EAN: 9783337222888

Printed in Europe, USA, Canada, Australia, Japan

Cover: Foto ©ninafisch / pixelio.de

More available books at **www.hansebooks.com**

COLONEL JOHNSON ENDEAVORING TO CAPTURE A REBEL OFFICER AT THE BATTLE OF PITTSBURG LANDING, BUT GETS ONLY A WIG.

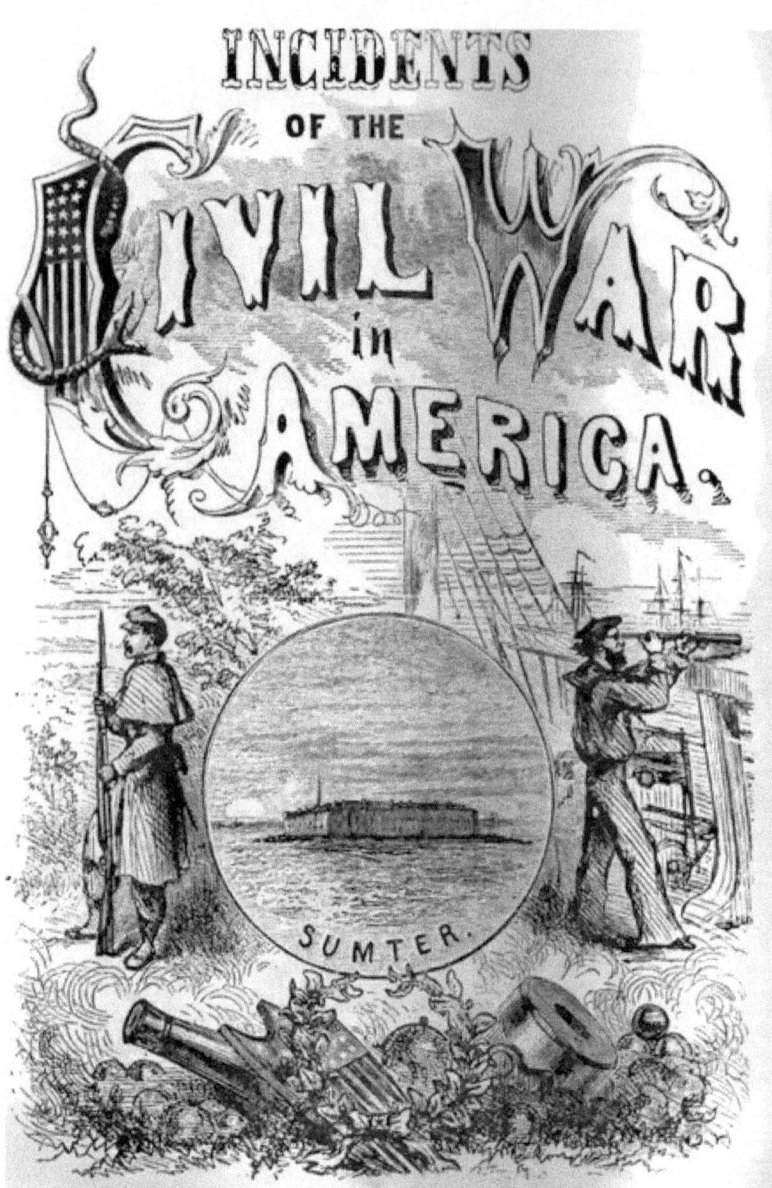

Entered according to Act of Congress, in the year 1862, by

FRANK LESLIE,

In the Clerk's Office of the United States District Court of the Southern District of New York.

HEROIC INCIDENTS,

Personal Adventures and Anecdotes

OF THE

CIVIL WAR IN AMERICA.

The Joan of Arc of Camp Dick Robinson.—A young lady who has been with the East Tennesseeans during their stay at Camp Dick Robinson, is thus alluded to by the camp correspondent of the Cincinnati *Times:* "One of the features of the 1st Tennessee Regiment is the person of a brave and accomplished young lady of but eighteen summers, and of prepossessing appearance, named Sarah Taylor, of East Tennessee, who is the step-daughter of Captain Dowden, of the 1st Tennessee Regiment. Miss Taylor is an exile from her home, having joined the fortunes of her step-father and her wandering companions, accompanying them in their perilous and dreary flight from their homes and estates. Miss Taylor has formed the determination to share with her late companions the dangers and fatigues of a military campaign. She has donned a neat blue chapeau, beneath which her long hair is fantastically arranged; bearing at her side a highly-finished regulation sword, and silver-mounted pistols in her belt, all of which gives her a very neat appearance. She is quite the idol of the Tennessee boys. They look upon her as a second Joan of Arc, believing that victory and glory will perch upon the standards borne in the ranks favored by her loved presence. Miss Captain Taylor is all courage and skill. Having become an adept in the sword exercise, and a sure shot with the pistol, she is determined to lead in the van of the march bearing her exiled and oppressed countrymen back to their homes, or, if failing, to offer up her own life's blood in the sacrifice."

A gentleman who was on the ground on Saturday night, the 19th instant, when the order was issued to the Tennesseeans to march to reinforce Colonel Garrard, informs us that the wildest excitement pervaded the whole camp, and that the young lady above alluded to mounted her horse, and, cap in hand, galloped along the line like a spirit of flame, cheering on the men. She wore a blue blouse, and was armed with pistols, sword, and rifle. Our informant, who has been at the camp the whole time since the arrival of the Tennesseeans, says that Miss Taylor is regarded by the troops as a guardian angel, who is to lead them to victory. These persecuted men look upon the daring girl who followed their fortunes through sunshine and shadow, with the tenderest feeling of veneration, and each would freely offer his life in her defence. There was but little sleep in the camp on Saturday night, so great was the joy of the men at the prospect of meeting the foe, and at a very early hour in the morning they filed away jubilantly, with their Joan of Arc in the van. Just before taking up their line of march they all knelt, and, lifting up their right hand, solemnly swore never to return without seeing their homes and loved ones. Whether the East Tennesseeans of Camp Dick Robinson shall do daring deeds or not, Miss Taylor's fame is perfectly secure. She is a girl of history, and poetry will embalm her name in undying numbers.

New Reading of an Old Fable.—The principal part of the fighting off the two forts below New Orleans, had been, at the commencement, done by the mortar boats. These had borne the brunt of the engagement, and so severe was the work necessarily imposed upon their officers and crews, that, had it been continued, they must have been forced to retire from sheer exhaustion. However, upon Wednesday, it was telegraphed that Commodore Farragut would certainly advance upon the following morning. When this became generally known, the crews, worn out by their labors during the day and the preceding ones, were overjoyed.

One of their commanders, however, did not seem to participate in the general feeling of pleasure.

"We've done the part of the cat,"—he grumbled, in the hearing of one of his subalterns,—"and now, hang it, the other animal is going to eat the roasted chesnuts."

It must be owned that the simile has some approximation to truth. But even if its truth were complete, it would scarcely be a politic expression. We may consequently, as well, omit specifying the number of the mortar boat, or the name of its commander.

Duck Shooting on the Mississippi.—When it had been determined on by the commander of the naval forces of the United States at the mouth of the "great river," then below forts Jackson and St. Philip, should pass them, and endeavor to run up to New Orleans, the *Cayuga* was one of the first gunboats that got under weigh. Hardly had she emerged from what one who was present named as "the perfect h-ll of fire that streamed upon her from the forts," and was gradually getting out of the range of their guns, than she found herself opposed by an actual swarm of Rebel gunboats. "They were as thick"—so one of her sailors said—"as Southern mosquitoes are in the Southern summer." There was no necessity for the commanding officer to beat to quarters, for the men were already standing at their guns. The Acting Master of the *Cayuga* bore the name of Morton. He was, as we understand, a New Jersey man, and hailed from the neighborhood of Bergen. In his youth he had been a "fast" boy, and considerably fonder of sport than labor, having been what sporting men would generally call, a crack shot. However, he had finally brought up in the navy, and had been commissioned, or rather named, to the position on board the boat, for we believe an Acting Master is not a commissioned officer. As he went round the guns he paused by the 11-inch pivot, bent down over it, and took a long and attentive squint at the enemy. Then raising and turning his head, he spoke to the men who were serving it:

"You see them, my boys, don't you!"

"Aye, aye, sir!"

"Now, look here, lads," he growled, "get the elevation neatly, and don't care one d—n about the range. We are duck-shooting, now. Plump it into the flock, and you're sure to hit some of them."

He was obeyed, and the result proved that he was right. As his commanding officer subsequently said, when speaking about this shot—

"No double-barrel ever scattered birds more beautifully."

"Boys! Never Mind Me."—The following incident came to us from an eye-witness who was on board the *Iroquois* during the bombardment of Fort Jackson. It is a fine example of gallantry and heroic self-abnegation, and deserves to preserve for the gallant sailor a bright page in the history of the period.

Midshipman or Acting Master Cole—we are unable to say which—was engaged in superintending the men while loading a gun. A grape-shot came through the side of the *Iroquois* while he was thus engaged and cut him down. It passed through his body and almost tore him into two. As he reeled back and fell, some of the gun's crew quitted it and sprang towards him. Motioning them away, he partially raised himself, resting upon his right arm on the spot where he had fallen.

"Boys! never mind me;" he faintly ejaculated.

"But you must be carried below, sir!" replied one of the men.

"No! What is the use? I'm going. Look—look after the gun."

He again fell back, and the men returned to their work. As he heard the report he once more looked up. "Did it hit her?"

"Yes, sir!"

The answer had fallen upon deafened ears. Scarcely had he shaped the last question than he had rolled backward upon the deck dead. Such a death as this is worthy of a niche in the memory of every true patriot.

The "Grit" of a Rebel.—It must by no means be supposed that all the gallantry and bravery of the nation is loyal to the Government. On the contrary, the South possesses a fair share of these qualities, and future historians will admit it as a paramount claim on the part of the North, that we were able to reunite our severed dominion in spite of the courage of our rebellious brethren.

Beverley Kennion, who was in command of the *Governor Moore*, one of the gunboats opposed to our fleet in the battle on the Mississippi below New Orleans, is, whatever his political and moral errors may be, a thoroughly brave and gallant man. When his craft was actually sinking, riddled like a sieve by the ordnance of the *Oneida*, Lee, who was in command of that gunboat, shouted out to him, pointing as he did to the Stars and Bars which were still streaming above her deck—

"I say there, haul down that d—d rag, will you?"

"No, I won't," yelled Beverley Kennion in return, "I'll see you in h-ll first." Improbable as the meeting thus proposed may be, none can deny that the sinking rebel showed his possession of considerable "grit," or will be disposed to regret that he had a chance prevented him, albeit against his will, of improving the acquaintance so agreeably commenced, in his subsequent compulsory visit to our fleet.

Rebels Caught in their Own Trap.—A private letter from a soldier in General Jameson's brigade, says: "Our division, or rather brigade, took 18 prisoners yesterday, down at Pohic Church. They were taken by Colonel Hayes, of the 63d Pennsylvania Volunteers, an active and efficient officer. The 63d were out on picket duty, and the attention of the sergeant of the guard being drawn to the tinkling of a cow-bell in the bushes, with visions of new milk running through his head, he examined carefully, and, to his intense astonishment, he found himself euchered of his milk, and no cows there, but he made the discovery that as he advanced, said cow-bell retreated. The sergeant smelt a moderate sized mice, and made a double-quick retrograde movement without investigating further. He immediately reported the fact to Colonel Hays. The Colonel secreted a squad of men in the woods, and Sergeant made himself conspicuous. Soon the gentle tinkle of a cow-bell was again heard. The Sergeant kept threshing in the bushes, and the bell gently tinkled, approaching all the while. Soon the squad in ambush had the satisfaction to observe the cautious approach, not of a cow, but of a veritable Secesher, with a cow-bell around his neck, and a 6-shooter stuck in his belt. He came slowly on until within easy range of our men. The Sergeant then hailed him, and asked him where he had rather go, 'to —— or to Washington.' 'To Washington, I reckon,' drawled the Secesher. 'I aint clothed for warm weather,' and he came up, without looking to the right or the left, and delivered himself up. He would have been looked upon as quite a hero by our men if the revengeful Secesher had not given information where the balance of his comrades were. That night company A, Pennsylvania 63d, went about six miles outside our pickets, and took 17 prisoners and 6 horses. One of the Seceshers requested the hostler to take good care of his horse, for he had had nothing to eat for two days."

Foraging in Fairfax.—Among the multifarious duties which fall to the lot of the soldier in an invading army is that of "foraging." It is sometimes not of a very pleasant nature, particularly when troops are from "sheer and inexorable necessity" compelled to levy upon the "goods and chattels" of the poor and humble and innocent as well as on the rich and criminal. The illustration opposite intelligibly sets forth the exploits of the soldiers; one mounted on a well-laden donkey who has docility portrayed in his demure countenance, the other alongside having been paying a visit to the poultry-yard of the rebel farmer. In war, "might constitutes right." The "boys" are elated at their success, and if we may judge from the hilarity and good nature which is so faithfully illustrated in the sketch, we may be fully assured that the prospect of dining on the fruits of their *legalized poaching* was to them equally as pleasant an idea as threshing a brigade of the half-starved Confederate forces. In the background of the picture are two other soldiers who have made a porcine levy, and are *en route* for camp. Foraging however has its two sides, and is by no means free from danger—*vide* the ready musket of its professor.

It is greatly to the credit of the United States army, that it has refrained as

FORAGING IN FAIRFAX.

much as possible from the foraging system, and has always, when compelled to make levies upon the effects of the enemy, shown a disposition to return a full value for it in specie,—not flimsy shinplasters, the "bogus" currency of the so-called Confederate States. From the fun and frolic usually attendant upon foraging, it is about the most pleasing portion of the active duties of the soldier in a military campaign. It calls into full play all his powers of adroitness, wit, and stealthy cunning, although he can go up to a farm-yard and select whatever his eye covets, with the same bold air of undisputed authority as the minions of a United States Marshal, when levying under an execution, he prefers to do it on the "sly" and create for himself a little notoriety in camp, and lay up a laugh and a story for after days. It should be stated that foraging parties do not confine themselves to the capture of mere *eatables*. Everything useful to an army is liable to be carried off—provender for horses and mules, is most needed and always secured, seeing that it is impossible to carry with the trains of an advancing army sufficient quantities of hay and oats for its beasts of burden.

The Drummer-Boy of Marblehead.—A lad of fifteen, is the hero of the story—showing that in the hearts of even the children of the North, the indomitable spirit of liberty throbs with an enthusiasm and courage, that quails not on the tented field, and is eager to do and to die for the country's flag.

Who can for a moment doubt the purity and success of the National cause, when we see the very *boys* of the Union, the darlings of the hearth-stone, tearing themselves from their mother's arms and from their weeping sisters, and foremost in the fight, beating their drums, or seizing, as in the case of Albert Manson, a rifle from a wounded soldier and firing on the foe, till falling faint and dying from a rebel ball? It was the murder of the Massachusetts troops in the streets of Baltimore, that roused the rage of his young heart to avenge their blood. Father and son, at once enlisted. The son could play the "Star Spangled Banner" and "Yankee Doodle," and on trial, Colonel Kurtz, struck with his bold and inspired manner, appointed him in one of the companies of the Massachusetts 23d, being the youngest drummer in the regiment.

They sailed in the Burnside expedition, and in the battle of Roanoke Island, after a weary march through slime and water, they came in sight of the enemy's battery. "Who will go and take it?" asked the general commanding. "The Massachusetts 23d," was the quick reply. "Forward, then, double-quick!" and in the teeth of a galling fire they rushed to their death as it had been to their bridal. The father fell wounded by his side, but the son heeded him not, his whole soul had lost itself in the work before him. "Look at that child," said one officer to another; "no wonder we conquer when boys fight so." "Didn't I say they should run to the old tunes?" and seizing a disabled revolver for a drum-stick, he struck up, in a wondrously defiant way, our impudent old strain of Yankee Doodle. A flying rebel heard it, and looking back, took sure aim at Albert. A man near the boy saw him, and tried to pull Albert down, but he stood his ground, and the ball did not fail to do its deadly work.

And you will love his knightly Colonel none the less when I tell you that his strong arms held the dying boy. His pale lips moved at last, and they bent eagerly to hear his words. Some inquiry for his missing father, some last precious words for his lonely mother? No; only this, boylike, "Which beat, quick, tell me?" Tears ran like rain down the blackened faces, and one in a voice husky with sobs said, "We, Albert, the field is ours." The ears death had already deadened, caught no sound, and his slight hand fluttered impatiently as again he gasped, "What, tell quick?" "We beat 'em intirely, me boy," said a big Irish sergeant, who was crying like a baby. He heard, then, and his voice was as strong as ever as he answered, "Why don't you go after em? Don't mind me, I'll catch up—I'm a little cold, but running will warm me." He never spoke again, the coldness of death stiffened his limbs, and so he passed from the victory of earth to the God who gave us the victory. If the mother of the Gracchi, could point to *her* sons and say "*these* are my jewels," with what a loftier, holier pride, can the Massachusetts mother of this gallant boy recall the memory of *her* heart's idol! Build him a monument of the old Bay State's granite, and let his name live forever, high in the temple of Fame!

Sequel of an Execution in the Rebel Army.—War, under all circumstances, is a terrible tragedy, but occasionally there springs from it an act so vengeful and bloody, in its conception and consequences, as to almost congeal our veins. There is an Irish company in the Confederate army called the "Tigers," from New Orleans. Two of them were recently shot for some disrespect to their "chivalrous" officers, construed into mutinous resistance. An account of the execution was published in the Richmond papers. As a result, in a letter from the camp, which appeared in the Nashville *Courier*, it is related: that, "yesterday morning, the bodies of two officers of the 7th Louisiana regiment were found with their throats cut. They were the officers of the day, and officers of the guard at the time of the commission of the outrage by the 'Tigers,' and were instrumental in bringing them to punishment. It would be well could the whole company be effaced for this new and most horrible villainy." Thousands of Irishmen were forced into the rebel ranks, in the summer, and it is probable enough they have no good will to the cause.

Capturing a Secession Wig.—*Frontispiece.*- Although the field of battle is by no means a mirthful spot, yet it is often the theatre of incidents which would provoke "a laugh under the ribs of death." General Burnett protests that the most comical spectacle he ever witnessed was that of an Irish soldier of his regiment in Mexico, suddenly called from foraging to fighting, charging heroically among the enemy with a white goose suspended across his shoulders, and flapping its wings helplessly across his back.

An incident serious enough essentially, but comical in its accessories, is related of Colonel Johnson, of the 28th Illinois regiment, at the battle of Pittsburg Landing. On the last day of the fight, when the rebel forces were flying in all directions, Colonel Johnson observed three rebel officers approaching the place where he was stationed. A cool and courageous man, he determined to make a capture, and dashing up to the fugitives, he fired his pistol at the nearest. The shot took effect, for the man fell forward in his saddle, which the Colonel imagined was merely a feint to escape another shot. He was not to be thus deceived, and darted up to the officer with the view of drawing him from his saddle by main force, at the same time seizing him by what he supposed was the hair of his head, but to his surprise and consternation he only brought away the rebel Major's wig! To complete his capture he made another plunge at the fugitive. It was, however, unnecessary, for the pistol shot had done its work, and the rebel officer fell a lifeless corpse from his saddle. Colonel Johnson says that to the latest day of his life he will not forget the incident, and the sight of artificial hair will always call to mind the death of the rebel major, and his inglorious capture of a secession wig.

Picketing on the Potomac.—Like most other duties connected with the active service,—and especially in an enemy's country,—picket duty has its pleasures and excitements, as well as its fatigues, its difficulties and its dangers. The scene represented in the opposite engraving is on the Potomac, where the Union army was compelled for a whole winter to hold extended lines of defence against the threatened invasion of Maryland. The picket guards for the protection of these lines were somewhat numerous, and at times within conversing distance of the enemy's pickets. Occasionally these had a friendly chat, and exchanged civilities. On one occasion an invitation was extended by a rebel to one of the Tammany regiment to meet him half way and join him in a mutual bumper of the inevitable whisky. The invitation was cordially accepted and mortal enmity temporarily dissolved. There is, however, in picket duty, much dull monotony and tedium. To relieve this tedium the pickets occasionally used to select each other as targets. Then the utmost caution was observed to keep the enemy in the dark as to position, range and every circumstance that could guide his aim. This is aptly illustrated in the sketch. The Union pickets are in the act of firing upon those of the enemy, each one behind his sheltering tree. One has been so fortunate as to obtain a rest for his piece. He has it placed through a hole in a tree and fires on his enemy safely and without discovery. Picket firing for *amusement* is not commendable, and the National war authorities very properly early issued orders for its discontinuance.

Scene at the Bombardment of Fort Pickens.—"The only man who was killed outright, during the two days' action, was an artilleryman, who was passing into the casemates with some bread from the bakehouse. A shell exploded at the other end of the area, and one piece, flying a distance of some two or three hundred feet, passed through his body under his arms. He walked a few steps and dropped dead. There are many almost miraculous escapes. A shell was heard coming toward a gun on the parapet, and the men dodged under their bomb-proofs. The shell hit fairly on top of the bomb-proof, went through and dropped into a pail of water beside the officer, where it exploded. When the men came out again to resume their work, all they saw of their officer was his heels sticking out of a pile of rubbish. After dig

PICKETING ON THE POTOMAC.

ging him out, they stood amazed to see that he was not even hurt. He rose up, shook the sand from his hair and clothes, and coolly said, "Come, come! what are you standing there gaping at? Load that gun there." At it they went again, as if nothing had happened. Another officer, who had charge of a battery of mortars, had no less than seventeen shells strike within ten yards of him. I saw the ground ploughed up in every direction, and yet not a man was hurt. About twenty of the men, who had been relieved from their guns, were sitting smoking and watching the firing in a corner, protected from shot by the walls, when half of a huge shell struck and buried itself right in the midst of the group, without disturbing them in the least. "What's that?" asked one. "The devil knows and he won't tell," indifferently responded another, and went on smoking. A 10-inch columbiad came rolling towards a group, the fuze whizzing and smoking. "Wonder if that will hit us?" "Guess not! we're too near it!" Crack! went the shell, flying in every direction, but fortunately escaping them all. The rebel powder was poor, as was also their shot and shell, except that portion which they succeeded in stealing before the rebellion broke out. Their practice, however, was said to be good—how could it have been otherwise? Uncle Sam taught them at his unparalleled school at West Point, but with little thought that the teaching would be thus employed.

A Young Knight of the West.—The zeal and alacrity with which the foreign element of our population, has rushed into the ranks of the army, is conspicuous amongst the Germans. Their strong love of freedom and free institutions, with their military knowledge and discipline, class that nationality amongst the bravest and best of our composite soldiery. As an instance of reckless gallantry, and fortitude under a most painful surgical operation, that of Hamilton, a son of Professor Leiber, is worthy of record. A Lieutenant of the 9th Illinois regiment, he was appointed aid-de-camp by General Halleck, for distinguished services at the bloody battle of Fort Donelson, where he was twice wounded. The first was a flesh wound, of which he made nothing. Presently, however, he was struck by a Minie ball in the same arm; this shattered his elbow, and the bones above and below, and he sank to the ground, fainting with loss of blood. He was picked up towards night, carried to a house, and thence, over a rough road, in an army wagon, to the river bank, a distance of three miles, which necessarily caused the greatest suffering. Arrived at the river bank, he was put on board a boat and conveyed with other wounded to a hospital, where his arm was amputated. When the operation was over the brave young fellow's first words were "How long will it be before I can rejoin my company?" No army, imbued with such a spirit, can be conquered; it may meet with a temporary reverse, but in the end *must* triumph.

McClellan and Beauregard in Mexico.—The subjoined narrative, by an intelligent Corporal in the service, when our great General Scott was pushing his way to the Halls of the Montezumas, is a proud compliment to the talents of the young Engineer, now at the head of the army of the Potomac. At a council of war, held just before the battle of the City of Mexico, a dispute arose between some Colonel and the Engineer-in-Chief; finally the Colonel said that there was a young Lieutenant in his regiment who had a correct chart of the defences, and the map of the demesne thereto adjacent. The Engineer-in-Chief sneeringly said, "*Very well*, sir, you had better send for *your* authority, and let us see this great map." The General nodded his approval, and the Colonel gave the name and address of the Lieutenant.

When we arrived at the General's quarters again, (says the narrator of the story,) the Lieutenant was introduced, and, at his colonel's request, produced his charts. The party were astonished at their finish and fine execution, and when, after examination, they were found to be perfectly correct, General Scott came forward, and grasping the young Lieutenant by the hand, personally complimented him on his skill, and thanked him for his efficiency. The Chief Engineer, somewhat chagrined at this display of learning on the part of his young rival, sneeringly said: "General, perhaps this young man has some plan by which this part of the defences may be attacked."

Upon inquiry, it was found that he *had* a plan, which was produced with some degree of reluctance and laid before the assembly. It was read and criticised, and corrected, and finally, to make a long story short, adopted. With some amendments by the council. This displeased the Engineer, who seemed to think that the Lieutenant, though but a few years his junior, had no right to display so much knowledge of a science which did not belong to his branch of the service.

"I need not tell you," continued the Corporal, "that, in the taking of Mexico a few days subsequently, the plan offered by this Lieutenant was of signal service, and that he was breveted soon afterwards."

Here the story ended, and the Sergeant relapsed into his "pipe and silence." We all looked for a while into the fire, when one of the sentinels asked him what was the name of this young Lieutenant. He slowly puffed the smoke from his mouth, and answered:

"I believe it was George—George B. McClellan."

"And who was the Engineer?"

"I believe his name was George, too—George T. Beauregard."

And we all smoked and looked, and looked into the fire, until the sentinel called out—

"Grand rounds! Turn out the guard!"

The Death of Colonel Ellsworth in Alexandria, Va.—The death of the lamented Colonel Ellsworth, the time and manner of that death—the promising character of the young martyr, and the unbounded patriotism which animated his every thought and action, have furnished materials for the eulogistic themes of the poet, the philosopher, the historian and the divine. The scene portrayed in the accompanying engraving is that which occurred after Colonel Ellsworth had torn down the secession flag which floated on the Marshall House in Alexandria, Va. The story of the capture of the flag is briefly told. The 1st New York Fire Zouaves, of which Ellsworth was commander, arrived in Alexandria, Va., on the 24th of May. Whilst taking immediate steps for stopping railway and telegraphic communication South, Colonel Ellsworth had occasion to pass through the principal street of Alexandria. He was accompanied by a single squad, with a sergeant from the first company of his regiment. On his way to the telegraph office, he noticed a secession flag floating over the Marshall House, kept by one J. W. Jackson. On reaching the Marshall House, he at once entered, and after demanding who had placed the flag there, but receiving no satisfactory reply, sprang up stairs, and reached the topmost story, whence by means of a ladder he climbed to the roof, and having obtained a knife from the military secretary of the regiment, cut down the rebellious emblem, and threw it at the feet of those who accompanied him. He did not tarry long; picking up the flag, the party next proceeded down the stairs, Private Francis E. Brownell first, Colonel Ellsworth next. As soon as he rounded a corner in the hall to descend the lower flight, a man leaped from a dark passage, and hardly noticing the private, levelled a double-barrelled gun square at the Colonel's breast. Brownell made a quick pass to turn the

COLONEL ELLSWORTH TEARING DOWN THE FIRST SECESSION FLAG IN ALEXANDRIA.

weapon aside, but the fellow's arm was firm, and discharged one barrel straight to its aim—the contents lodging in the heart of the Colonel, who fell forward on his face, his blood perfectly saturating the secession flag, which he was carelessly rolling up as he descended the stairs. Quick as lightning Brownell avenged his Colonel's death, discharging his rifle in the assassin's head. Ignorant of the fatal effect of the wound which he had inflicted, he next thrust his sabre-bayonet through the assassin's body, the force of the blow sending the dead man, who proved to be Jackson, the keeper of the hotel, violently down the upper section of the second flight of stairs, at the foot of which he lay in his blood.

Then occurred a scene of agony. A woman rushed wildly from an inner room, gave one hurried glance at the body of the dead assassin, and then cried

DEATH OF JACKSON, THE MURDERER OF ELLSWORTH.

aloud with an agony so piercing, so heartrending that no person could witness her distress without emotion. She flung her arms in the air, struck her brow madly, and seemed in every way utterly abandoned to desolation and frenzy. It was her husband who had been slain. Although maddened to despair she yet listened to what was said to her. The soldiers did all they could to soothe her wounded feelings, and made her fully sensible that the safety of her children, for whom she expressed great fears, could not possibly be endangered. Such was an opening incident of the war between the loyal men of the North and treasonable rebels of the South.

Brother against Brother.—One of the most melancholy features of our sad, civil war, is the disruption of family ties, and the array of relatives and kindred against each other in deadly strife. Former friendships are forgotten, the altar of home abandoned, and bitter hate usurps the place of past affection. The highest and most distinguished households of the land, are no exceptions.

Hon. John J. Crittenden, for example, has a nephew, (Brigadier-General Thomas L. Crittenden,) loyal like himself, now commanding an important division in the National army, while another son (George Crittenden) is a Major-General in the rebel service.

So the eldest son of Kentucky's great advocate for the Union was recently arrested for treason, while his brother, Thomas H. Clay, is stated to have preferred the complaint on which the arrest was made, while a nephew, young Henry Clay, is an Assistant Adjutant-General in the Union army.

Prominent among the leaders and organizers of the Union party in Kentucky is the well-known George D. Prentice. His son, Clarence Prentice, is an officer in the rebel army, which lately threatened that its first work in Louisville, after taking possession of the city, would be to hang the father.

Ex-Governor Helm was recently arrested for treason. His cousin is one of the most reliable Union men now assisting the central column of the National army by their knowledge of the country and the people.

The venerable Robert J. Breckinridge only the other day published a masterly defence of the government, in a crushing denunciation of the traitor leaders of rebellion. Among those traitors his scarcely less distinguished nephew, ex-Vice President John C. Breckinridge, has a prominent place, is a Brigadier-General, and is now at the head of a brigade, with the avowed object of subjugating his native State.

Ex-Governor Wickliffe but yesterday urged the expulsion of a colleague charged only with sympathy with the rebels. His own son, is in the rebel army. And so the list might be extended indefinitely.

The Steamer "City of Alton" Saved by a Woman.—Among the many deeds of lofty daring in these dark and bloody days, lovely, impulsive, patriotic woman, comes in for no small share. Indeed, a volume might be written of her heroism, which would put to blush the valor and endurance of the sterner sex; like a guardian angel, sometimes, in the hospital, we see her wiping the death-damp from the soldier's brow; and sometimes at the peril of her own life, as in the instance we are about recording, warning our brave boatmen in the West of the hidden foe.

On approaching Commerce, the mate, who was on the watch, saw a woman, Mrs. Eversoll, on the bank, gesticulating violently, surrounded by a few men, and ever and anon her two little girls would tug at her dress as if to induce her to keep quiet. The mate was uncharitable enough to think that the woman had been indulging in liquor, and knew not what she did; but there was "method in her madness." The mail was to be put out, and wood to be taken in, and despite the continued waving of the woman's hand northward, the boat stood into shore. At last the boat was about to touch the shore, and the plank was half way over the bow, when the mate heard her exclaim, "Go back, go back! Jeff. Thompson is here with his soldiers!" Captain Barnes at this moment rushed out of his room, coat and boots off, to find the boat backing out and the balls plunging into his room and all around. He then saw the full force of the assailants springing up from behind the wood pile, and rushing like madmen down a lane towards the bank of the river.

The boat swiftly sped to an island below. The lady who saved the boat, and probably many lives, deserves a testimonial. Let her have it speedily.

Divine Service on the Flag-Ship Benton.—It is a beautiful tribute to religion, to see our gallant officers and hardy seamen bending the knee of homage to the God of battles; the capstan is the pulpit, covered with the "Union Jack," whilst our illustrious Commodore and Christian, the heroic Foote, reminds the men to be prepared for death, and the duties of the holy Sabbath in the worship of the Most High.

He offered up a prayer from the Episcopal service. While praying "Our Father, who art in Heaven," the report, and zip, zip, zip of a shot or shell from the enemy's guns could be distinctly heard by all present. But calm and unmoved, he eloquently and feelingly progressed with the service until concluded. Just as he had finished, the Quartermaster reported that the enemy had opened from a couple of their batteries. Their shots, however, fell harmless, and out of range.

Enlistment Incident.—At Newport, Rhode Island, (God bless the generous little State!) a young man had enlisted, and had gone to his mother to obtain her signature to his certificate. It was a hard struggle for her to give up her only boy, but she consented at last upon the condition that he should thrust his finger at random through the leaves of the closed Bible, and the language of the text upon which it rested should decide her action in the matter. He did as she requested, and his finger, when the Bible was opened, was found resting over the 2d Book of Chronicles, 20th chapter, 16th and 17th verses: "To-morrow go ye down against them; behold, they come up by the cliff of Zis; and ye shall find them at the end of the brook, before the wilderness of Jerusalem. Ye shall not need to fight in this battle; set yourselves, stand ye still, and see the salvation of the Lord with you. Oh, Judah and Jerusalem;

EFFECT OF CANNON SHOT AT PITTSBURG LANDING.

fear not, nor be dismayed; to-morrow go out against them; for the Lord will be with you." The mother read and consented.

"**Recapturing Oneself.**"—The incidents of the personal daring and romantic adventures developed in this war would fill a volume; nor is the fact remarkable when we regard the immense territory over which the conflict is spread. Although forming but one grand Republic, each State has something peculiar in its thoughts and habits—the cool, calculating Eastern man—the indomitable Western farmer—the impulsive Kentuckian and the fiery Tennessean—all these act differently under the same circumstances, and yet all tend to the same result. Two incidents lately happened exemplifying the National presence of mind. On the 18th of April, Lieutenant Edward K. Mull, of Captain Wash-

"RECAPTURING ONESELF."—CAPTAIN FRAZER, OF THE 21ST MASSACHUSETTS, TURNING THE TABLES UPON HIS REBEL CAPTORS.

ington Richards's company, 3d regiment Pennsylvania Reserves, while on duty near the Rappahannock river, was captured by a party of rebels, and carried off some distance, where a guard, armed with a shot gun, was put over him to prevent him from making his escape, while the party went to look for more game. As soon as the captors were out of sight, the Lieutenant pulled a revolver from his coat pocket, and holding it close to the head of his guard politely informed him that he would be under the painful necessity of blowing his brains out if he did not instantly lay down his gun and go with him. The frightened rebel obeyed orders, and it was not long before the Lieutenant was back in his own camp, as good as new, accompanied by his prize. Lieutenant Mull is a native of Berks County, Pennsylvania. The other, which is illustrated on the preceding page, is still more extraordinary. Captain Frazer, of the 21st Massachusetts regiment, having been taken prisoner during the assault on the rebel works at Newbern, was convoyed away under an armed guard of three rebel soldiers. Arriving at a favorable spot in the woods, he coolly remarked to the guard, pretending at the same time to draw a revolver from his side pocket: "There must be some mistake about this—now come along with me, you are my prisoners." Astonishing as this may sound, Captain Frazer actually brought his three captors as prisoners into camp. Our readers will agree with our artist that such a triumph of daring deserves the compliment of an illustration.

A Modern Toussaint L'Ouverture; Adventures of Potomac Jim.— When Colonel Graham of the 5th Excelsior regiment made his daring reconnoissance of Mathias Point, in November, 1861, a considerable number of negro slaves, the property of rebel masters, took advantage of his return across the Potomac to escape from bondage. A part of the camp was appropriated to their use, where they built log-huts, and obtained their support through services rendered to the officers and soldiers. In time they secured large accessions to their numbers, until the "Contraband Camp" contained nearly one hundred and fifty "fugitives from labor." They were mostly men and boys, with strong attachments for their relatives remaining in the "House of Bondage," whom they were anxious to have join them under their new conditions and relations. Many stories are told of the daring efforts made by some of them to bring off their wives and children from the Virginia or rebel shore. Among these perhaps the most remarkable is that of James Lawson, better known as "Potomac Jim." He was the slave of a Mr. Taylor, living near Hempstead, in Virginia, and made his escape early in December, 1861.

After reaching the National camp he shipped on board the *Freeborn*, flag-gunboat, Lieutenant Samuel Magaw, commanding. He furnished the Captain with much valuable information concerning the rebel movements, and from his quiet, every-day behavior, soon won the esteem of the commanding officer.

Captain Magaw, shortly after Jim's arrival on board the *Freeborn*, sent him upon a scouting tour through the rebel fortifications, more to test his reliability than anything else; and the mission, although fraught with great danger, was executed by Jim in the most faithful manner. Again Jim was sent into Virginia, landing at the White House, below Mount Vernon, and going into the interior for several miles, encountered the fire of picket guards and posted sentries, returned in safety to the shore, and was brought off in the Captain's gig, under the fire of the rebel musketry.

Jim had a wife and four children at that time in Virginia. They belonged to the same man as Jim did; he was anxious to get them, yet it seemed impossible. One day in January, Jim came to the Captain's room and asked permission to be landed that evening on the Virginia side, as he wished to bring off his family. "Why, Jim," said Captain Magaw, "how will you be able to pass the pickets?"

"I want to try, Captain; I think I can get 'em over safely," meekly replied Jim.

"Well, you have my permission;" and Captain Magaw ordered one of the gunboats to land Jim that night on whatever part the shore he might designate, and return for him the following evening.

True to his appointment Jim was at the spot with his wife and family, and were taken on board the gunboat and brought over to Liverpool Point, where Colonel Graham had given them a log house to live in, just back of his own quarters. Jim ran the gauntlet of the sentries unharmed, never taking to the roads, but keeping in the woods—every footpath of which, and almost every tree, he knew from his boyhood up.

Several weeks afterward another reconnoissance was planned, and Jim sent with the party composing it. He returned in safety, and was highly complimented by Generals Hooker, Sickles, and the entire flotilla.

Sometime in March, it became necessary to obtain correct information of the enemy's movements. His batteries at Shipping and Cockpit Points had been evacuated, and his troops moved to Fredericksburg. Jim was the man picked out for the occasion by General Sickles and Captain Magaw. The General came down to Colonel Graham's quarters about 9 o'clock in the evening, and sent for Jim. There were present the General, Colonel Graham, and the writer. Jim came into the Colonel's tent.

"Jim," said the General, "I want you to go over to Virginia to-night, and find out what forces they have at Aquia Creek and Fredericksburg. If you want any men to accompany you, pick them out."

"I know *two* men that would like to go," Jim answered.

"Well, get them, and be back as soon as possible."

Away went Jim over to the contraband camp, and returning almost immediately, brought with him two very intelligent looking negroes.

"Are you all ready," inquired the General.

"All ready, sir," the trio responded.

"Well, here, Jim, you take my pistol," said General Sickles, unbuckling it from his belt, "and if you are successful, I will give you $100."

Jim hoped he would be, and with a hearty good-bye, started off for the gunboat *Satellite*, Captain Foster, who landed him and his companions a short distance below the Potomac creek batteries. They were to return early in the morning, but were unable, from the great distance they went in the interior.

Long before daylight on Saturday morning the gunboat was lying off the appointed place. As the day dawned, Captain Foster discovered a mounted picket guard near the beach, and almost at the same instant saw Jim to the left of them, in the woods, sighting his gun at the rebel cavalry. He ordered the "gig" to be manned and rowed to the shore. The rebels moved along slowly, thinking to intercept the boat, when Foster gave them a shell, which scattered them. Jim, with only one of his original companions, and two fresh "contrabands," came on board. Jim had *lost the other*. He had been challenged by a picket when some distance in advance of Jim, and the negro, instead of answering the summons, fired the contents of Sickles' revolver at the picket. It was an unfortunate occurrence, for at that time the entire picket guard rushed out of a small house near the spot, and fired their muskets at Jim's companion, killing him instantly. Jim and the other three hid themselves in a hollow near a fence, and after the pickets gave up pursuit, crept through the woods to the shore. From the close proximity of the rebel pickets, Jim could not display a light, which was the signal for Foster to send a boat.

Captain Foster, after hearing Jim's story of the shooting of his companion, determined to avenge his death; so, steaming his vessel close in to the shore, he sighted his guns for a barn, where the rebel cavalry were hiding. He fired two shells—one went right through the barn, killing four of the rebels and seven of their horses. Captain Foster, seeing the effect of his shots, said

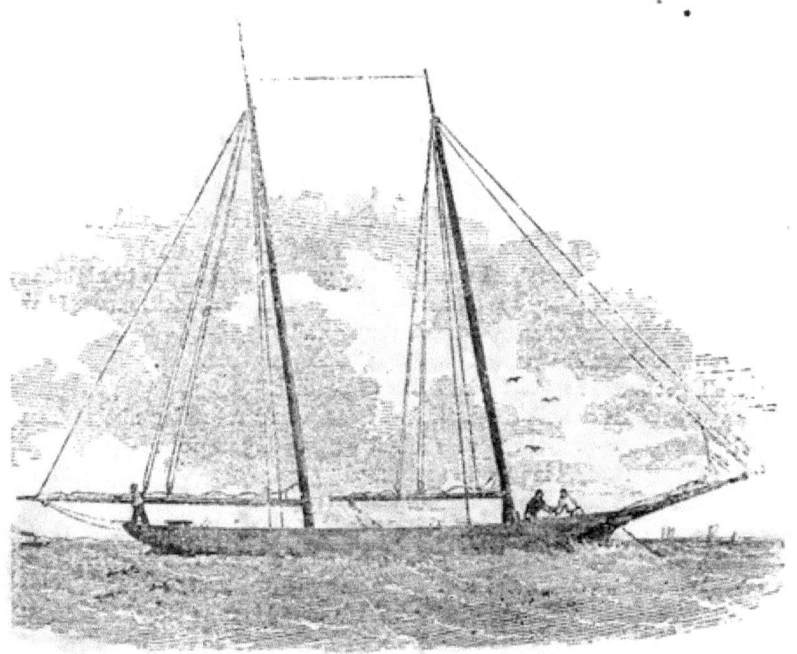

SCHOONER ALERT, CAPTURED OFF FERNANDINA, BY U. S. GUNBOAT BIENVILLE.

to Jim, who stood by: "Well, Jim, I've avenged the death of poor Cornelius," (the name of Jim's lost companion.)

General Hooker transmitted to the War Department an account of Jim's reconnoissance to Fredericksburg, and united with the army and navy stationed on the left wing of the Potomac, in the hope that the Government would present him with a fitting recompense for his gallant services.

The "Look-Out" near the Post-Office, Hilton Head, S. C.—Few people unacquainted with camp life, can form anything like an adequate idea of the innumerable inventions, of which Necessity is the mother, for the purpose of securing a force in the field against surprise. The engraving shows how fully alive the Union forces were to the danger of their position at Hilton Head, where a look-out was established from the top of a tall tree, whence the movements of an enemy could be discovered miles away, and whence the approach of the mails from the North were duly announced. To a soldier engaged in actual warfare, the arrival of the mail is an event of the greatest moment. He rushes to see if his friends and acquaintances have remembered him in his absence, and is glad to hear the news from home. Contemplating the sketch below, one can readily imagine with what anxiety the watch stationed in the look-out elevates his glass to discover the true character of the distant vessel which he

THE "LOOK-OUT," NEAR THE POST-OFFICE, HILTON HEAD, S. C.

discerns, a speck on the distant horizon, reporting to the guard below the result of his telescopic observations.

Carson the Scout.—Among the killed at Pittsburg Landing was "Young Carson the Scout," a man of wonderful daring and energy, reckless of danger but prudent, acute, active and intelligent, rivalling in all these qualities his namesake of the Plains and Rocky Mountains. His name in full was Irving W. Carson. He was born in Scotland, although in *physique* he was a true type of the men of the North-west. He emigrated from his native country, then a mere youth, to Chicago, Illinois, in the year 1853, and obtained employment in the Illinois Central Machine-shops. Subsequently he left the building and repairing of engines to run them, and for a long time faithfully fulfilled the duties of an engineer upon the above road. Naturally roving in his disposition and undecided as to his calling, about two years since he changed avocations abruptly and singularly and entered a law office in Chicago, as a lawyer's clerk. He was a faithful student, rose rapidly in his profession, and about the time the war broke out was admitted to the bar. Nature, however, had not destined him for the forum, and it is a matter of doubt whether he would have succeeded in the practice of his profession. At the first call for volunteers, young Carson abandoned his calling and enlisted as a private in Barker's Dragoons, in which company he received his first lessons in the school of war. Subsequently he was attached to General Prentiss' staff as a scout, at Cairo, then went into the same service under General Grant, whose confidence he enjoyed thoroughly. General Grant entrusted to him the most delicate and dangerous missions, all of which he fulfilled to the very letter of his instructions. At the time of his death, he had just returned to General Grant with the intelligence that General Buell's reinforcements were coming up, delivered his message, stepped back, and that instant a cannon ball took off his head.

Carson was about six feet two inches in height, very slight, but well knit, sinewy, alert, and handsomely formed. His face was thin, and bronzed by exposure to all kinds of weather, his cheek bones high and prominent, his eyes large, black and piercing, and his hair, which he always wore very long, as as black as a raven's. He combined in his personal appearance the peculiarities of an Indian with a native Southerner, a fact which was of great advantage to him in his scouting expeditions among the rebels. He was very taciturn and non-communicative, even among his friends, made little conversation, and appeared and disappeared like a flash. Vidocq himself could not have been more mysterious. We have known him to retire early in the evening, and would find him in bed early in the morning, and yet during the night he had ridden many miles. He was seldom absent any length of time, as his expeditions required the utmost dispatch. We have known him to come into the room, hastily seize his saddle, spurs and pistol, mount his horse—and he was a splendid horseman—dash off in a direction no one ever thought of taking, and only a few hours after would be strolling about the St. Charles like some awkward rustic just in from the Egyptian swamps.

His trip to Columbus, Kentucky, was an instance of the manner in which he accomplished his duties. He rose early that morning, arrayed himself in a rough homespun suit of blue—a style of clothing which alternates with the "butternut" among the rebels—rowed across the Ohio to the Kentucky shore, tied up his skiff and struck off through the woods and swamps until he reached a corn-crib, near which a wagon and pair of mules were standing. Carson rapidly loaded the wagon with corn from the crib, jumped aboard and drove off at a rapid pace for Columbus. He reached the town about 10 o'clock in the forenoon, having passed the enemy's pickets without trouble, and came rattling down the bluff behind the town at a merry pace. The rebel General Polk confiscated the wagon, corn, and one of the mules, magnanimously allowing him the other to return with. Before leaving, however, he obtained permission to go through the fortifications, the rebels little dreaming of the real character of the awkward Kentucky farmer they were admitting into their works. He spent two or three hours upon the bluff, ascertained the number of guns, their calibre and range, a rough estimate of the forces, and made a diagram of the spot while in the water battery. He ate dinner in one of the log houses used as barracks by the soldiers, and about 2 o'clock left the town upon his mule, with his thumb upon his nose, and fingers gyrating Columbus ward. At 8 o'clock the same evening he was sitting in the supper room of the St. Charles, at Cairo. We were present when our forces occupied Columbus, and found his diagram was correct in all its particulars. The same diagram appeared in many papers after the evacuation, to the correspondents of which he had furnished it.

He was present at the battle of Donelson as General Grant's special courier. Upon the Sunday when the rebel Buckner sent in his flag of truce, he was ordered to go to the right wing and tell General Wallace, General McClernand and Colonel Oglesbe to storm the works of the enemy at once. In a letter written to a friend in this city, which we have before us, alluding to this order, he says: "I never went with a despatch to any place in my life faster than I did with that one. I felt as if I wanted to see the last man wiped out. I have got a natural hatred for traitors, and never intend to let any chance slip when I can dispose of them in a decent way."

After the battle he found many letters in the rebel camp. Among them was one from an interesting young woman in the Southern part of Tennessee, writing to her brother, desiring him to capture a live Yankee and send him to her for a pet. On one of his scouting expeditions, some time after, he made it in his way to call upon the identical young lady. He went to the house and inquired for the damsel that wanted a pet. She soon made her appearance. He told her he had been captured at Fort Donelson by her brother, and had been sent to her as a pet, and very politely informed her he was at her service. The young woman looked horrified and said there must be some mistake. Carson said there was not; that he was going to live South in the future, and more than that, was bound to be her pet, and would make himself as useful as possible, strongly intimating that she might do the same by getting him some dinner. The young woman, scared out of her senses, complied, and furnished him an excellent meal, during which he showed her the letter, and informed her that her brother was a prisoner in the Federal camp. Young woman went into hysterics, and the whole family commenced a sort of Tennessee dance. By this time his arrival was noised about in the neighborhood, and as preparations were making which looked to an unpleasant state of things for Carson, he mounted his horse and was off and out of sight not a minute too soon for his safety.

His hatred of traitors was most bitter and intense—when he did speak of them it was only to denounce them in the most violent terms. Even in his sleep he would toss about restlessly and mutter his denunciations. One night we distinctly remember at the "St. Charles," when he jumped from his bed and frantically rushed about the room, cursing secessionists and thrusting his cutlass into the bureau, chairs and wall with desperate strength. The next instant a correspondent lying in another bed was horrified to behold him rushing at him and thrusting the cutlass into the sheets, at the same time expressing a vigorous determination to rid the world of one more traitor. Correspondent was out of the sheets and under the bed in a twinkling. It was a long time before Carson was awakened to a realizing sense of what he was doing. After that no one was especially desirous of sleeping with him.

The last letter he ever wrote was to a lady in Chicago, and is as follows:

SAVANNAH, March 26th, 1862.

MY DEAR FRIEND,—Your note of March 17th was handed to me last night in General Grant's headquarters. I have been absent for eight days. I went with despatches from this place to find General Buell. I was ignorant of his whereabouts, but made up my mind to keep going until I found his division. I kept on until we came to Columbia, Tenn., just 150 miles from this place. In traversing this distance I was obliged to pass through three secession camps. As everything depended upon my getting through safely, I came to the conclusion that I would make the trip or get down to New Orleans in trying. After four days' ride I got to Nashville, some 200 miles from this point. I felt as if a feather bed would not hurt me in the least, but to my surprise I was ordered to return to General Grant with my despatches. I mounted a pretty nearly worn-out horse, and again set out to brave whatever dangers might lie in my path. For a long distance we passed off for secession soldiers, and got along finely till we reached Columbia. In coming to this place, the Southern soldiers had been through the town and the bridge had been destroyed across Duck river, which obliged us to leave our horses in a livery stable. In the meantime, the secesh soldiers came into town, and made inquiries as to where we left our horses. I came to the conclusion that they would catch me and get my despatches, which would give them just the information they needed. They placed men all around the town for the purpose of catching me. I had only two men with me and one of them did not amount to much. I told them I was going to run through or burst up in business. We moved on very slowly till we came close on to them. I put spurs to my horse, the other two doing the same, dashed through the stream, and got through safe. They chased us for a long distance, but we soon left them far behind. . . . .

OF THE CIVIL WAR IN AMERICA.

PICKET STATION OF THE NEW YORK 34TH REGIMENT ON THE UPPER POTOMAC.

We are expecting a battle soon. Perhaps, after the fight, *if I do not get killed*, I will make a visit to Chicago. Hoping to hear from you soon, I remain your true friend, I. W. CARSON, Major-General Grant's Scouts.

Poor Carson's presentiment was realized. His mutilated body was sent to Chicago, where it was interred, as was befitting, with military honors. His valuable services rendered at all times in the most imminent danger, will secure for him a lasting and grateful recollection as one of the youthful martyrs of the war.

Secession at Home.—One of the most dauntless and truly eloquent defenders of the Union is the Hon. Andrew Johnson, United States Senator from Tennessee, to whose trumpet-tongued appeals many of us have listened with delight, as he went through the country urging the people to loyalty, and filling the hearts of traitors with fear and trembling.

In a speech at Columbus, Ohio, he depicted the outrages of the rebels in East Tennessee in the following glowing and soul-stirring language:

"This, my friends, is secession, and these are the men you are to 'compromise with.' Some of the same demons, five of them, fiends in human shape, stopped at the house of a man named Markham, who, seeing them approach, and fearing insult and outrage to himself, if he remained, and thinking that they would not be so likely to provoke a quarrel with the family if he were not present, took his rifle from its resting place and retired unobserved by them into a little thicket hard by the house, in order to be at hand in case they offered any abuse to his family. He had an amiable wife and two daughters, the youngest a girl of about 12 years, and the other just blossoming into womanhood, about 16, and as beautiful as the morning and as pure as the dewdrop. The secessionists entered and insolently demanded dinner for themselves and feed for their horses. The wife told them there was the crib and the fodder, and they would give them their dinner. They took the hay and the corn and scattered it about the ground, and ordered the ladies to hasten their dinner.

"In due time the meal was prepared, and soon greedily devoured. After sating their appetites at the table, they began to address rude remarks to the wife and daughters. One attempted to make love to the young lady, when her young sister, seizing the tin horn or trumpet, which is kept in almost all rural homesteads to make a summons to dinner or sound an alarm to the neighbors in case of an accident, sprang to the door and blew a blast. At this the hellish demon turned, drew a pistol from his girdle, fired its bullet through her brain, and with one wild shriek she fell in agonizing death at the feet of her screaming mother. That blast, the shot, the shriek and scream, pierced the ear of the waiting father; he sprang from his retreat, he stood at his door—one glance revealed all; and taking deliberate aim, he sent his rifle's bullet straight through the villain's heart! The other four, alarmed at the trumpet's blast, and knowing that the whole neighborhood would soon be upon them, mounted their horses and fled. The enraged father, finding them beyond his reach, turning to where the slayer of his daughter lay, seized his axe and cut his brutal body into quarters and threw them out as only fit for the dogs to devour!

"Such, my friends, is secession at home. It is robbery, rapine and murder. And it is marching towards you, and will be upon you. You must arm for your own defence. I speak not to you in fables. These things occurred not in a remote country, but right over there in Tennessee. I seem even yet to hear the shriek that went up from that young and innocent heart as it took leave of life, so wild, so clear, so agonizing, that even angelic spirits might come to listen and avenge! Will not you, then, rush to the support of your government and the rescue of your country from the reign of terror that has no parallel in the history of civilized man?" Let it be preserved as a truthful and horrible memento of rebel atrocities.

The Zouave and the Virginian.—Much has been said against the Zouaves —that they were a mere set of banditti, the scum of cities, etc., and perhaps some of them are—but that they gallantly avenged the death of the brave Ellsworth, their Colonel, at Bull Run and elsewhere, cannot be denied, and we like to give honor to whom honor is due. As the anecdote we relate comes from the correspondent of the Charleston *Courier*, we cannot doubt its authenticity, and only wonder he was frank and generous enough to publish it.

He says, "Among the prisoners at Richmond is a noble-looking and intelligent Zouave, one of the few decent exceptions in the crew. I saw him on the field, just after he was taken. While passing a group of our men, one of them called him some hard names. 'Sir,' said the Zouave, turning on his heel and looking the Virginian full in the eye, 'I have heard that your's was a nation of gentlemen, but your insult comes from a coward and a knave. I am your prisoner, but you have no right to fling your curses upon me because I am unfortunate. Of the two, sir, I consider myself the gentleman.' I need not add, that the Virginian slunk away under the merited rebuke, or that a dozen soldiers generously gathered around the prisoner and assured him of protection from further insult."

Virginia Bushwhackers.—The guerilla mode of warfare is very popular in the Old Dominion, and a source of much annoyance to National troops. They go in squads of 10 or 20, being organized by confederate authority, and provided with ammunition for their old flintlock squirrel rifles. In their gray homespun breeches, speckled flannel shirts, and slouch hats with a white cross on the crown, provided with rations, they push for the cliffs and jungles. Woe to the unlucky horseman or footman in Union uniform who passes within 150 yards of their unerring rifles. He falls as sure as a trigger is pulled. It matters not whether the victim is flying with courier speed or at rest by the roadside, if a bushwhacker "draws bead" on either, the swift ball wings its flight fatally, and the soldier dies. Not unfrequently they let fly at a moving column, and all efforts to catch them are futile. They aim from the top of a rock, and before our swiftest footmen can clamber to their position they disappear in the jungle.

The figure of a bushwhacker is as ungainly and forbidding as a toothless, freckled slattern. I have seen many, but **never a striking** person among them. Their bodies are long, spare, bony and sinewy, and they are as fleet as antelopes,

LARGE GRAINED POWDER USED IN RODMAN'S 15 INCH GUN.

and capable of great endurance. Their features are thin, rugged, sunburned and bewhiskered, and their hair is long and tangled as the thickets in which they prowl. And their habits and movements are sly, suspicious and cunning.

Large Grained Powder for Rodman's Gun.—It is well known that Captain Rodman, U. S. A., is the inventor of a system of casting guns of a heavier calibre than are known in the Old World, whereby the cooling of the metal when cast is so managed as to secure a solidity and strength unattainable under the old process. Captain Rodman has cast several 15-inch guns, and is now engaged on others of 20 inches bore, calculated to throw a shot of half a ton. It is believed that a single shot from one of these guns would utterly demolish any of the boasted iron-clad frigates of England or France. They are not intended so much for range as power, battering or crushing power, and this is best effected at a comparatively low velocity. To secure this, Captain Rodman has resorted to the use of powder in large grains, some of which, of full size, are represented above. Europe has by no means kept pace with the United States in heavy ordnance, as she will discover in the first collision.

A Yankee Trick in Missouri.—The Yankee is not only up to tricks in trade, but knows how to play them off in war too, when he wants to trap a secessionist. Among the most cunning as well as successful, is one told of Major Hovey, practised near Clinton, Missouri. It was at the time when our Federal trains were so frequently attacked and captured by roving marauders lying in ambush on their route.

Anticipating such a contingency to him, the Major took 100 men, put them in wagons, so as to hide them from view, and then putting a few stragglers to walk, as if guarding the train, he started out. Secession, shot gun in hand, hiding in the brush, saw the cortege, and supposed it a federal wagon train poorly guarded, and hence an easy as well as legitimate prize. Reasoning thus, secession walked from the bush, presented its shot gun, and demanded a surrender—which demand was instantly met by fifty men rising from the wagons, presenting a row of glittering muskets, and requesting a similar favor of astonished and now mortified secessionists. They generally complied, and worked off its ill-humor by cursing such "mean Yankee tricks," unknown to all honorable warfare, and unworthy of chivalrous hearts.

Destroying the Telegraph between Fort Pulaski and Savannah.—One of the coercive measures adopted by the National troops against Fort Pulaski, after cutting off communication between the fort and Savannah, by means of batteries judiciously placed on the banks of the Savannah river, was to interrupt the telegraph running through the reed-covered island to the city. This task was performed by Captain Budd and a detachment of sailors from the United States gunboat "Ellen." The sailors, accustomed to climb the mast

DESTROYING THE TELEGRAPH ACROSS THE MARSHES BETWEEN SAVANNAH AND FORT PULASKI.

sprang up the telegraph poles, and being armed with hatchets, the wires were soon severed from the insulators, and suddenly the operators at Savannah lost the thread of their conversation with the defenders of Pulaski. The task completed, all communication between the city and the fortress was cut off. This service had a most important influence in enabling the expedition sent against Pulaski to effect its purpose without much bloodshed.

A Female Spy.—No doubt the sunny South has received many, and some very important, favors from the fair sex. At Washington, for a while, they played an almost open game, being in several instances educated, handsome and fashionable, having access to cabinet circles, and intimate with heads of bureaus, officers of war, State, etc. A pretty and talented woman is a dangerous article to the peace of man individually, and sometimes to the peace of the country. Even patriotism is not safe against the charms, and wiles, and intrigues of the gay deceivers.

Therefore it was that our generally gallant Secretary of State felt compelled to arrest and imprison, first in their own houses, and afterwards in less comfortable quarters, a few of the most dangerous of the sex. At last a well-known lady, was detected in corresponding and receiving messages through the medium of pound-cake, which circumstance determined him to ship them all to Norfolk by a flag of truce, as the only way to get rid of such a nuisance.

The heroine of our chapter is a Mrs. Baxley, who was arrested and examined on the steamer Georgiana between Fortress Monroe and Baltimore.

From some remarks she made, a Mr. Brigham, who was a detective, jocosely asked her if she was a secessionist, to which she answered, "yes." After the gang plank was run out, the boat having landed at Baltimore, Mrs. Baxley was heard to say that she "thanked God she had arrived home safe;" and when about stepping ashore Mr. Brigham tapped her on the shoulder and requested her attendance in the ladies' cabin. As soon as the room was reached her bonnet was taken off, between the linings of which was found upwards of fifty letters sewed in, when she exclaimed that having been found out, she thought it best to deliver up the "contrabands" and be allowed to proceed on her way. But Mr. Brigham insisted upon it that she had others, and lo! in her shoes and stockings numerous other letters were also found. The lady was closely guarded until the Provost Marshal of Baltimore was informed of the circumstance, when he sent a woman to examine Mrs. Baxley with more scrutiny. Almost every possible place about her clothing was filled with letters from Secessia for rebel sympathizers in Baltimore, but in her corsets was found a document which, when taken by the woman examining the smuggler, Mrs. Baxley rushed at her, and getting hold of the paper, tore it in two. The document proved to be a commission from Jeff. Davis to a Dr. Septimus Brown, of Baltimore, also passes and directions for him to run the federal blockade in order to gain the rebel domains.

Mrs. Baxley was taken to a hotel and several police officers placed on guard over her. While locked in her room she dropped a note out of the window addressed to her lover (the rebel doctor), imploring him for God's sake to fly, as all was discovered. It seemed to be her only and darling desire to get her lover a commission in the rebel army, and, having succeeded, she was only detected in her nefarious transactions when about completing her mission.

Strange Facts and Fortunes of the War.—In an interesting letter from Newbern, from a gentleman whose name is familiar to many of the reading public, the writer states that he has on his hands to feed, shelter and clothe, and find occupation for over 1,000 negroes, men, women and children. He says he has 230 able bodied men to breakfast, each of whom receives $8 a month from Government. They are mostly kept at work on the trenches. In addition thereto he has nearly 60 families of whites who were actually starving. "Is not that getting in the rear of the enemy," he asks, "when we are in his home supporting his wives and children?" He further states:

"Yesterday I had an application for support from the widow of a late United States Major-General, the wife of an officer who had served in the Mexican war, and she was the daughter of a Colonel in the war of 1812. At the very same time there was a poor escaped slave knocking at the door for the very same assistance.

"Many of the white people are very poor and ignorant, and, I think, the most pitiable objects of charity I have ever seen. As a white man, I am ashamed to say they are really more abject and degraded than the blacks. I never realized so much before the *dignity* that the mere ability and willingness to labor gives a man. The blacks having always been forced to work, although lazy, generally ask for and go to work; while, too often, the white, having been taught to regard work as degrading, allows himself to sit in laziness and sink down into utter helplessness.

"The consequence can easily be imagined; in a time like the present, he who can and will work is getting it to do, and with it its reward, prosperity and plenty; and they who will not (or 'cannot') become dependent. Most of the negro women get work at the hospitals, washing and the peddling of cakes, and earn a support in this way. We gave them a lift at first with a few pounds of flour, and so far, immediately on their arrival, they have been able to find a house to live in. When they arrive it is usually in groups of 10 or 20, often all from one plantation.

"They have travelled, in some cases, long distances. I had one poor negro of about 25 years of age who had come over sixty miles. His feet were all bloody, and the first thing he could do after he had reported his name for work, and had a breakfast, was to lie down and sleep; for two or three days he was quite sick. At the end of that time he went to work, and is now doing his best to support the United States government with 'de shobel and de hoe.' He gave valuable information to the government."

What General Cass has done.—Few if any of our millionaires have been more generous with their purse in aid and comfort to our volunteers than General Cass, the statesman and veteran of the north-west. Too old to join in person at their head, as it was his pride to do in his younger days, he neverthe-

36   HEROIC INCIDENTS AND ANECDOTES

"CONTRABAND" CULVERT UNDER THE CHESAPEAKE AND OHIO CANAL, NEAR THE MOUTH OF MUDDY BRANCH, POTOMAC RIVER, A PASSAGE FOR SMUGGLERS.

less has mounted his uniform of 1812, and reviews the troops congregated in Detroit, every morning. Not only has he contributed out of his private fortune upwards of $25,000 to the thorough equipment of the Michigan troops, but has lately added the munificent sum of $10,000 to the support of their families during their absence from home.

Contraband Culvert.—"Muddy Branch is the name of a small but deep tributary of the Potomac, entering that river about 30 miles above Washington. It is crossed on a broad culvert by the Chesapeake and Ohio Canal, beneath which the rebels were accustomed to hide their boats in their secret correspondence between Virginia and Maryland. The hiding place was finally detected, and the rebel sympathisers of Maryland cut off from communication with their friends in "Secessia."

The Palmetto Flag.—The Palmetto flag is that of the seceding State of South Carolina. The Palmetto is a species of dwarf Palm, and reaches its highest latitude in that State. During the war of the Revolution, a fort of Palmetto logs was built for the protection of Charleston harbor, on the spot now occupied by Fort Moultrie, which effectually beat off the English fleet. For this and other reasons the Palmetto was adopted as a symbol in the arms and on the flag of South Carolina.

THE PALMETTO FLAG OF CHARLESTON, S. C.

The Camp Disease.—That there is much painful and distressing sickness in both the National and rebel armies is a melancholy truth. Go to the hospitals and see the pale, wounded soldiers, moaning on their pallets, and the spectacle will make the sympathetic tear trickle down the sternest cheek. But it seems from the confessions of the Alabama volunteers that a new disease prevails there, happily not known in the Northern sick-lists. We will not undertake to describe its symptoms, as we trust our surgeons will never have occasion to prescribe for such patients, but give rather as a curiosity to our readers the language of the poor fellow who was attacked with it in common with many others around him.

"The first symptom is a horror of gunpowder. The patient can't abide the smell of it, but is seized with a nervous trembling of the knees, and a whiteness about the liver, and a longing inclination to advance backward. That's the way water serves mad dogs. Then comes what our Major calls home fever; and next the sufferer's wife and nine children are taken sick; after which the poor fellow takes a collapse, and then a relapse. But it's mighty hard to get a discharge, or even a furlough—awful hard. Fact is, you can't do it without working the thing pretty low down. I tell you what, Bob, between you and me, I'm afraid I'm taking the disease myself; I don't like the reports we hear every day from the coast. We hear cannon booming down there by the hour, and they say the Yankees are going to playing the very devil with our ducks. I think I can detect a faint smell of powder in the breeze, and feel a strange desire to go into some hole or other. It may be the climate; I hope so, but don't see how that should make me turn so cold about the haversack every time I see a bayonet. If I only had some good spirits now, to take every morning, I think I could stand it very well. Please send me some immediately on receipt of this. (N. B.—Mark the box 'Drugs, care Surgeon 2d Battery Alabama Volunteers.') Our Major is sharp as a briar, and down on brandy like a duck on a June bug."

Scouts and Spies.—If the exploits, the disguises, the subterfuges and adventures of the secret service of the two armies were written, they would equal the Romantic Chronicles of Fouché himself.

In Washington, it was not difficult for the rebel authorities to find ready agents, tinctured as it was with secession prejudices and proclivities, from the departments and public bureaus down to the hotels, bar-rooms and stables. The National countersigns, it is notorious, were sent to the enemy even before they were known to the loyal guards and pickets. One of the most successful and popular characters assumed has been that of pretended refugees from the enemy. They had sacrificed every thing, stocks, houses and farms, and were homeless paupers—all for the Union. But General McClellan, by a rigid system of demanding proof of their declarations, finally put a stop to this sort of emigration.

Another numerous class were the pedlers and venders about the camps and cities, who, while they were selling cakes and stationery, and sometimes, it is said, even tracts and Bibles, occupied themselves with cunningly prying into the strength and appointments of an entire division.

The scout, however, is a character of quite another order. The spy is generally unarmed, trusting to stratagem and an artful tongue, while the brave scout, with his rifle in his hand and pistol in his belt, is always ready to take a life or lose his own. Many, as solitary Rangers, are now serving the Union cause in Virginia and Tennessee; others are detailed to enter the enemy's territory, but we hear little of their expeditions, dangers and discoveries, as they must be kept secret at headquarters.

If the white steed and sinister rider, which attracted so much attention at the affair of Ball's Bluff, have been a source of mystery and supernatural lore to some of our troops, we have given the rebels an equivalent in the "Spectre Scout," a mysterious being which is said used to haunt the woods below Leesburg, in the vicinity of the river. The actual facts of the case are, that a number of rebel pickets were shot on their posts thereabouts, generally without any marks being left of a struggle, and with no clue as to the author of the deed, except that suggested by an occasional glimpse of a tall and swift-moving figure in the neighborhood. Without wishing to disturb any pleasant ideas of the weird and unearthly the matter may have afforded, it may be presumed that the mysterious personage aforesaid, whoever he might have been, was merely some "Yankee" who had lost a brother or other relative at the Ball's Bluff massacre, and undertook to perform the part of an avenger on his own account, and in a manner in accordance with the popular conception of the character. Of the reality of the existence of this singular destroyer of the rebels there is no doubt or mistake whatever.

Romantic Marriage.—The ladies of the land enter heart and hand into the humanities of the war. Thousands to-day are plying their busy needles, some knitting socks, and others making shirts and drawers, whilst many are preparing and forwarding jellies, comfits and delicacies to their brave fathers and brothers or sons on distant battle-fields, or lying sick and weary on beds of pain. A large number too have volunteered their services as nurses for the hospitals—and it is here that we see woman in her loveliest office as an angel of mercy, soothing the pangs of the wounded and noiselessly flitting from one to another like a devoted sister; ministering the cool drink to the parched lip, as she whispers hope and consolation to the sinking sufferer. There is more than one Miss Nightingale in our camps, who has dedicated her life to the cause of our country.

In the 25th Massachusetts regiment, a young and educated lady, Miss Wheelan, has been adopted as Daughter of the Regiment, and has accompanied it in all its long and tedious marches.

As hospital nurse she has made herself a universal favorite amongst the officers and men. To Captain Emory, of Company B, she became particularly endeared. Amid the toils of camp life and the duties of a soldier, he found time to cultivate a more especial friendship and affection. The result was romantic—the marriage of Miss Wheelan to Captain Emory took place in the city of Newbern. The ceremony was performed by the Rev. Mr. Hart, Chaplain of the 3d New York artillery, and was honored with the attendance of Generals Burnside, Reno and Foster, and many other officers and friends. During the evening they were serenaded by the band of the 25th Massachusetts.

Thus does sly little cupid steal into the camp of Mars, and with one of his invisible arrows, brings the stalwart warrior to surrender at discretion, a willing captive to the omnipotence of love. "None but the brave deserves the fair."

Tarring and Feathering Mr. Kimball.—It is the duty of every loyal citizen to inculcate, both by precept and example, habits of peace, law and order. Circumstances, however, occur from time to time when a member of a community persistently challenges the public indignation, and the ordinary forms of justice are dispensed with, in order that the penalty shall be not merely prompt but heavy. It was this state of feeling which gave rise to Lynch Law, and the still more antiquated system of "tarring and feathering." It is a method of punishing criminals which belonged more peculiarly to the South and West than to the North of the United States. The loyal people at Haverhill, Mass., in the month of August, 1861, became indignant at the treasonable conduct of Mr. Ambrose M. Kimball, editor of the *Essex County Democrat*. For some months he had published in his paper a series of violent articles in favor of secession. Not content with publishing the treasonable speeches of Breckenridge and Vallandigham, he gave "aid and comfort" to the rebels by the most violent denunciations of the Union and its defenders. On the evening of the 19th August, the smothered indignation of the populace burst forth, and a committee waited upon Mr. Kimball, asking him to apologise, recant, and no longer outrage the sentiments of the public. This he decidedly refused to do. He was, thereupon, taken down Main street, in front of the Eagle House. A

TARRING AND FEATHERING MR. KIMBALL, EDITOR OF THE ESSEX "DEMOCRAT," HAVERHILL, MASS., A REBEL SYMPATHISER.

FACSIMILE OF A NOTE ISSUED BY THE STATE OF SOUTH CAROLINA.

spectator gives the following description: "After removing every article of clothing but his drawers, he was completely covered with a coat of tar and feathers, after which, being mounted on a rail, or pole, was conveyed to Merrimac street, in front of the office of the *Democrat*, and directly under the American flag, behind which, as with a 'masked battery,' he had bombarded the Government of his country. He was required to cheer the flag, which he did; after which the crowd moved in the direction of Bradford. On arriving at the bridge he was allowed to dismount and walk through it, when he again mounted the rail and was carried to the residence of George Johnson, Esq., who was called out, but the nature of the exercises there we were unable to learn. Returning to town, a halt was made in front of the Eagle House, when the question was again submitted, if he regretted his conduct, to which he replied in the affirmative; when, by request he knelt down, and, raising his hand, repeated in substance the following confession and affirmation: 'I am sorry that I have published what I have, and I promise that I will never again write or publish articles against the North, and in favor of Secession, so help me God.' After this he was conducted to his home."

The engraving accompanying the foregoing sketch represents Mr. Kimball in the act of undergoing the unpleasant ordeal which the citizens of Haverhill imposed upon him.

Twenty-Five Cent Southern Shinplasters.—Not the least difficulty which the rebel leaders had to encounter was the want of money, to raise, equip, maintain and pay their armies. Without something in the shape or form of money it would have been impossible for them to make a move. Accordingly recourse was had to the expedient of circulating "Shinplasters." We give a *facsimile* of those issued by the Bank of the State of South Carolina, for the munificent sum of twenty-five cents. As an illustration of the working of the Shinplaster system, we make a few extracts from a recent work entitled, "Prison Life at Richmond." The author says :—" One of the most important duties attendant upon prison life is the purchase of articles necessary for comfort and health. For this purpose a negro was placed at our disposal, whose ingress and egresss was allowed at all hours of the day. An officer, let it be supposed, desires to purchase a woolen shirt, one pair of woolen drawers, two pair of woolen stockings, one pair of cassinette pants, all of them of the same quality as those furnished by the United States government to the privates in the army. After waiting patiently for a day or two, before he can catch the darkey, he at last secures him, places in his hands twenty dollars in gold with a memorandum of the articles, and away the darkey starts. Next day, perhaps in the afternoon, he returns with the following bill :

One Woolen shirt $4 25
One pair Woolen drawers 4 00
Two pair Woolen stockings 1 50
One pair Cassinette pants 9 00

Total 18 75

The cost in the Federal States 6 45

But the darkey brings change to the amount of $1 25 which is handed to the officer in the following notes, many of them faded and torn.

One Bill, Corporation of Richmond .... 50 cts.
"   "   "   Petersburg ....•..... 25 "
"   "   Farmer's and Savings Bank................. 10 "
"   "   Corporation of Winchester.................. 10 "
"   "   "   Frederick .... 5 "
"   "   Confederate House, (tavern bill private)....... 10 "
Two Bills Southern exchange, private issue .... 15 "

Total eight notes $1 25

Proceeding, the writer remarks, " this is a matter of daily occurrence ; and, as a new comer among us receives a roll of bills, too extensive for his pocket book, it is amusing to see his stare of wonder and surprise, as he slowly unfolds the roll, smooths them out, and scans them one by one,—looks at the darkey, then at the nearest prisoner, who perhaps comes to his rescue, informing him that it is good 'Secesh' money, that four of those notes will buy him a pound of sugar, or ten of them will purchase a quire of tolerably good writing paper. When the darkey makes his appearance in a store, he is immediately recognized as the agent of the Yankee prisoners, the tariff goes up, and gold is expected in payment for his purchases. Distressed as are the residents of Richmond by speculators and the blockade, the poor Yankee suffers still more ; for the negro makes his profit as well as the store-keeper. Yet the Confederate soldier fares as badly as the Yankee, according to the following extract from a Centreville camp letter, published in a Richmond paper:

"By paying five prices for the article, you obtain anything in the market from sardines to stove polish. Oysters arrive every night fresh from the shell, only $1 per quart; boots $25 per pair, etc. We are assured that all the specie circulating in Richmond is distributed by the Yankee prisoners. It commands 50 per cent premium. Of course we receive none when our purchases are made." In the same work—"Prison Life at Richmond," we find the following story taken from the Richmond *Dispatch*. "Leaning over the counter, a volunteer was endeavoring to reckon the change just paid out by the sleek-haired clerk. Before him lay a quantity of mutilated bills—ragged and dirty pieces of paper, bits of cardboard, printed checks, a few copper pennies, milk tickets, postage stamps, and other interesting specimens of the present outrageous 'coin of the realm.' Over and over again the puzzled volunteer essayed to count the pile of outrageous currency, and over and over again he failed to find it satisfactory. It was too much for his rustic arithmetic; the problem was too much to solve upon only ten fingers. The bystanders laughed. The money was spread out upon a show case as young ladies lay cards upon a table in telling fortunes, and the soldier stood before it searchingly examining every piece. 'Do you call this money?' he asked, taking up a small yellow parallelogram, looking very like the brass card of a sardine box; 'Do you call this money?' (holding up an advertisement of fine Havana segars) 'and this?' —a bill for fifteen cents on which some weak-minded printer had gone raving mad, in different kinds of type—"Good for one shave." Reading slowly— "Dick the barber." 'Do you call this money?' The sleek-haired clerk was puzzled also. 'It will pass all over town, indeed it will, sir.' Once more the soldier scrutinized the ragged and incongruous pile and grasping it in one hand, soliloquized 'So this is money? money eh! I call it stuff; why a man might hold his hand full and then have but thirty-seven and a half cents money.'"

Landing Reinforcements on Santa Rosa Island for Fort Pickens.— One of the first objects of earnest solicitude with the Government of the United States, on the secession movement becoming a great fact, was the reinforcement of Fort Pickens. Three large steamers, one of them the Powhattan of eleven guns, were dispatched for that purpose, carrying nearly 900 officers and soldiers, together with large supplies of arms, ammunition, provisions, horses, etc., etc. The task of landing on Santa Rosa Island was a delicate and difficult one, inasmuch as the Confederate forces at Pensacola and Forts McRea and Barrancas outnumbered the National troops nearly six to one. The accompanying engraving shows the troops in the act of swimming their horses to land, which duty was performed most successfully during the afternoon and night of the 18th of April, without a single casualty. The scenery depicted by the artist shows that at that time, particularly at night, Santa Rosa Island had a drear and desolate aspect, and that the task of landing the horses in the manner set forth,

RELIEVING FORT PICKENS—LANDING HORSES FROM THE UNITED STATES TRANSPORTS.

DARING RIDE OF COLONEL LANDER AT THE BATTLE OF PHILIPPI.

was by no means an inviting or pleasant one. The whole affair of reinforcing Fort Pickens was admirably done.

Daring Ride of Colonel Lander at the Battle of Philippi.—There is hardly any officer connected with the United States Army—regular or volunteer—who justified so many wonderful stories of deeds of intrepidity and daring, as the late gallant Colonel Lander. His career was full of that excitement which constant and secret danger creates, and the unceasing watchfulness necessary to guard against sudden surprises, had made him at once cool in his recklessness, and equal to any and every emergency. In the battle of Philippi he displayed a daring spirit and extraordinary presence of mind. In reaching the brow of the hill overlooking Philippi, he beheld the enemy, and at the same moment observed the advancing column of Colonel Kelley. Without the delay of a minute he had planted his cannon to play on the rebel camp, and without either fear or thought of the danger, only thinking of the necessity of communicating with his brother officers, he put spurs to his horse and dashed down the face of the hill, the descent being at an angle of forty-five degrees. The accompanying engraving shows the perilous character of the ride. So dangerous was the feat that Colonel Lander's men gazed after him with hushed breath until they saw him reach the base in safety and dash across the town, accomplishing most successfully all the objects which he had in view.

Uncle Sam First.—There are many anecdotes and bon-mots connected with the war that are too good to be lost. The love of country in preference to any and everything else—business, home and parental obligations, has never in any other national contest, been so universally prominent. All classes, trades and professions, the lawyer and politician, the parson and the poet, the blacksmith and the plough-boy, have hastened to crush the viper, Rebellion, and restore the Union.

Among the stories told of the Massachusetts 8th is the following:

"As soon as the Massachusetts regiment had made prize of the ferry-boat (on the Susquehannah), a call was made for engineers to run her. Some twenty men at once stepped to the front. We of the New York 7th afterwards concluded, that whatever was wanted in the way of skill and handicraft could be found among those brother Yankees. They were the men to make armies of. They could tailor for themselves, shoe themselves, do their own blacksmithing, gunsmithing, and all other work that calls for sturdy arms and nimble fingers. In fact I have such profound confidence in the universal accomplishment of the Massachusetts 8th, that I have no doubt, if the order were, 'Poets, to the front!' 'Painters, present arms!' 'Sculptors, charge bayonets!' a baker's dozen out of every company would respond."

Before the departure of the Brooklyn regiment, a man who carried on the blacksmithing business with two of his sons, concluded to enlist.

Next day down comes the oldest of the boys. The blacksmith's business "wasn't very driving, and he guessed John could take care of it." "Well," said the old man, "go it." And the oldest son went it. But the day following John made his appearance. He felt lonesome, and had shut up shop. The father remonstrated, but the boy would enlist, and enlist he did. Now the old gentleman had two more sons, who "worked the farm," near Flushing. The military fever seems to have run in the family, for no sooner had the father and two elder brothers enlisted, than the younger sons came in for a like purpose. The father is a man of few words, but he said that he "wouldn't stand this, anyhow." The blacksmith business might go to the d—l, but the farm must be looked after. So the boys were sent home. Presently one of them reappeared. They had concluded that one could manage the farm, and had tossed up to see who should go with the 14th, and he had won the chance.

This arrangement was finally agreed to. But on the day of departure the last boy of the family was on hand to join, and on foot for marching. The old man was somewhat puzzled to know what arrangement could have been made which would allow all of the family to go, but the explanation of the boy solved the difficulty. "Father," said he, with a confidential chuckle in the old man's ear, "I've let the farm on shares!" Father and four sons, went with the 14th regiment.

But one of the best and most laconic, is that of a farmer in Wisconsin, whose son had joined the 8th regiment without his consent.

Several letters were written, persuading him to return; at last the father wrote him that he must come—that he had a large amount of threshing to do—that he could not afford to hire help, if it were to be had, which was hardly possible, owing to the number of enlistments—and that he must return home and help him, even if he enlisted again afterward. The young man replied:

"DEAR FATHER,—I can't go home at present. I should be very glad to help you, but Uncle Sam has got a mighty sight bigger job of thrashing on hand than you have, and I'm bound to see him out of the woods first."

The Flag of Fort Sumter.—History will record that when citizens of the American Republic first fired upon the symbol of their own nationality, they fired upon the Flag of Sumter. Eighty-six years before, when the armed patriots of Massachusetts met the soldiers of their oppressor, on the little village green of Lexington,

"They fired a shot heard round the world."

Not less significant was the shot that, booming across Charleston Harbor, bore to all the world tidings, strange and dreadful, of a people revolting against themselves. The elder nations looked and listened—at first with amazement, afterwards with joy. For in that act—sacriligious and wicked—they saw, or thought they saw, the destruction of the Model Republic. Throughout our own land, as news of the dreadful deed burned along the wires, men held their breath, not less in wonder than in passionate indignation. Even in the rebel city of New Orleans stores were closed, and pale faced citizens went about in silence, or whispered together in little knots at the street corners, overwhelmed with a consciousness of great wrong committed against their country. A brief delay—and then the whole loyal people of the North rose up as one man and rushed to the battle-field, there to wash out in blood the insult offered by traitors to the sacred flag of the Republic. How dreadful has thus far been the punishment of treason the world already knows. But it will be yet more dreadful before all is ended. The Flag of Sumter! Not a wound in that dear old banner but shall be avenged tenfold on the treacherous and barbarous hordes of a wicked rebellion. So I reflected, looking upon its torn and tattered folds, when, after the bombardment, the gallant Anderson brought it away with his brave command. Well and nobly had they defended it! I have made you a little sketch of this memorable token—memorable now and for all after time. Thank God it still waves over the country it has so long blessed!

"Yet, Freedom, yet thy banner torn but flying,
Streams like a thunderstorm against the wind."

THE FLAG OF FORT SUMTER, AS IT APPEARED AFTER THE BOMBARDMENT.

The Wreck of the Governor.—It was night. The sky, which had all day been dark and lowering, was now black with threatening clouds. The wind rose, lashing the waves to a white foam, and as they beat about our vessel greatly impeded her course.

We were half a day out from Fortress Monroe, bound for Port Royal, and our little craft was not such as could weather so rough a sea. When built she had been intended for river navigation, but on this occasion was employed as a transport, and had on board a battalion of marines, under command of Major John George Reynolds.

At first no serious apprehension of danger was entertained by any of our

RESCUE OF MAJOR REYNOLDS'S BATTALION OF MARINES FROM THE FOUNDERING STEAM TRANSPORT GOVERNOR, BY THE OFFICERS AND CREW OF THE UNITED STATES FRIGATE SABINE.

party. But the night grew darker; the black clouds sent forth lightning flashes from their inky bosoms, and the rain fell in a ceaseless pour.

Every moment the storm increased in intensity. Our brave commander, though a firm and fearless man, looked pale and anxious. The dread grew contagious, and though I don't believe there was a coward among us, we all looked doubtfully on the dark waves, the red glare of lightning, and the almost blinding rain. Under the increasing fury of the storm our vessel began to roll fearfully. The waves beat against the bulwarks and stove them in. Our fires were put out, and great confusion on board now increased our disheartening prospect. Presently a leak was discovered, and from that terrible moment all efforts to preserve order were useless. The scene that followed was most heartrending. We were of those who held ourselves ready to give up our lives at any moment. But to die thus ingloriously—mere victims of a storm at sea! We had none of us reckoned upon this, and so death wore its most dreadful guise. Yet escape seemed impossible. How we all stood, pale and horror-stricken, waiting for the final crash! How impossible it seemed, as, from time to time we looked in each other's faces, to realize that in a few minutes we would all be struggling hopelessly with the furious waves that looked eager to suck us into death! How, amid it all, a glimmer of hope would spring up within our hearts that we might yet be saved! Then as the deadly peril of our situation rose before us more vividly, how it would leave us more hopeless and despairing than before! But what is that dimly seen through the darkness?

Ah! God of the storms and the winds and the waves! It is a steamer that heaves in sight! For a moment this appearance of rescue stupefied us; but in the next a gun, signal of distress, boomed across the angry waters. Another moment and it is answered. Oh, but our breathes come quick, as minute by minute the good Sabine draws nearer—and when at last she throws out a hawser, our grateful hearts make strong our arms to draw it in and fasten it securely. Then comes our perilous escape!

One by one we cast ourselves on that friend, and, hand over hand—a painful and tedious work—make the journey from our lost vessel to the frigate. I was among the last to get on board in safety, but I watched with an anxious heart the progress of my comrades—for it was a matter of time to reach the Sabine—and now and then a weary hand would lose its hold of the hawser, and some poor fellow would, unheard, fall into the water beneath; then after struggling a little while with the merciless waves sink beneath them, and be seen no more.

It was a dreadful scene. The black sky overhead; the fitful lightning; the roar of the angry waves,—the trembling terror of the timid, the solemn bearing of the brave—all was here of danger and of sublimity that could fix an image in the memory forever. Nor shall I ever forget how, when we were all on board the Sabine, the hawser was cut away, and, while we yet silently watched her lights, and now and then by the fitful glare caught a glimpse of her hull and rigging, the shattered transport sank away into the dreadful abyss of ocean, from which we had been snatched as by a miracle.

Chat with a Contraband.—If the amusing incidents and dialogues with the "darkies" in Secessia, could be compiled, they would form a rare and unique volume. We seldom hear the genuine dialect in the North, and know but little of the real nature of the regular plantation, thick-lipped, bow-legged biped.

There is a vein of humor and comical conceit, running all through his conversation, which is altogether "*sui generis.*" Out of a number, we select a description of an accidental interview in the Green river country, Kentucky, between one of our officers and a leader of a group of Ebonies, coming up a hill.

First were two intelligent looking contrabands, next, a little "go-cart," drawn by a mule, in which was a female slave and about a dozen little negroes, carefully wrapped in sundry cast off coats. An Uncle Tom sort of a chap, with a Miss Dinah, brought up the rear. As they came by, I addressed Tom : " Well Uncle, where did your party come from ?" " We's from de town dar, sah." " And where are you going ?" " Gwine home, sah." " Then you do not live in the village ?" " No ; we lib right ober yonder, 'bout a mile ; de secesh druv us from home." " Ah ! well now stop a minute, and tell me all about it." " Dat I do, sure, massa. Jim, (to the other leader of the mule cart,) you go on wid de wagon, an' I kotch you fore you gits home. Now I tells you, massa, all about um. My massa am Union, an' so is all de niggers. Yesterday massa wor away in de town, an' de firs' ting we know, 'long come two or free hundred ob dem seceshers on horses, an' lookin' like cut-froats. Golly, but de gals wor scared. Jus' back ob us wor de Union soldiers—God bless, (reverentially,) for dey keep de secesh from killin' nigger. De gals know dat, an' when dey see de secesh comin' dey pitch de little nigger in de go-cart, an' den we all broke for de Union soldiers." " So you are not afraid of the Union soldiers ?" " God bless you massa, nebber. Nigger gets ahind dem Union soldiers, secesh nebber gets um. Secesh steal nigger—Union man nebber steal um. Dats a fac', massa.".

General Mitchell and Mrs. Polk.—There are many stories told of the haughty, disdainful, and at times coarse and insulting receptions of the National troops, by the female rebels of Dixie.

In Alexandria, and Nashville too, the so-called ladies would on the streets turn up their little noses in disgust when meeting a United States uniform, and when their windows were not closely barred, sometimes would there manifest their spite in modes no way delicate. Our men, to their credit, instead of resenting these insults, as a rule quickly march on or only laugh at the impotent rage directed against them. Sometimes, however, it has been found proper, if not necessary, to administer a rebuke ; and the reply of General Mitchell to to Mrs. Polk, widow of the late President, is a model to be copied, as a courteous and at the same time severe reprimand to feminine insolence.

One day, General Buell and all his Brigadiers went in a body, to make a call on Mrs. Polk and her niece. The gentlemen simply bowed on presentation in silence, until General Mitchell who was standing apart was singled out. To him Mrs. Polk remarked : " General, I trust this war will speedily terminate by the acknowledgment of Southern independence. The remark was the signal for a lull in the conversation, and all eyes were turned upon the General to hear his reply. He stood with his lips firmly compressed and his eyes looking fully into those of Mrs. Polk as long as she spoke. He then said: "Madam, the man whose name you bear was once the President of the United States; he was an honest man and a true patriot; he administered the laws of this Government with equal justice to all. We know no independence of one section of our country which does not belong to all others, and judging by the past, if the mute lips of the honored dead, who lies so near us could speak, they would express the hope that this war might never cease if that cessation was purchased by the dissolution of the Union of States over which he once presided." It is needless to say the effect was electrical, made, as the remark was, in a calm, dignified tone and with that earnestness for which the General is noted; no offence could be taken. Southern independence was not mentioned again during the interview.

Colloquy between Pickets.—Habit is second nature in war, as well as in peace, and often after a few days' exposure to the perils of picket service, the men seem to forget all danger, and convert the tragedy of being shot into a jocose comedy. Here is an illustration:

"Pick out your trees and let 'em have it, boys," said Captain Trounsteine. Our men were quickly in position behind their natural fortifications. "Come out o' there, ye d—n Yankees," shouted a concealed butternut. "What for you no come out?" shouted a Teutonic Federal. "You be d—d?" replied a chivalry, seconding his words with a rifle shot, which made a number of our men think a blue bottled fly was in close proximity to their ears. "You'd better not show that secesh head o' yours," shouted a 5th cavalry man. "Stick out yer abolition mug if you dare," replied the butternut. This interesting kind of conversation was kept up until dark, when it ceased on both sides.

A Fighting Clergyman.—In the days of the Revolution our ministers preached and prayed patriotism from their pulpits; in the holy work of putting down the rebellion many of our parsons have abandoned their gowns and desks and flocks, and entered the army.

We read a week or two ago of a zealous pastor in Wisconsin whose soul was so full of the war, after the news of the Pittsburg retreat on Sunday, that instead of opening the services as is customary with "Let us pray," he actually said, "Let us *drill*."

It is recorded too of Rev. Wetmore, of Connecticut, when word of a great victory was handed to him while preaching, he drew himself up, and announcing it to the congregation, said, "My friends, the house of God is no place for boisterous demonstrations, we will therefore, in giving *three cheers*, only go through the motions." That they were given with an emphasis the reader will easily imagine.

The Rev. B. C. Ward, of Illinois, believes it to be his duty to abandon the pulpit for the field. He proposes to raise a company of clergymen only—

PICKET DUTY, STATION OF THE 4TH NEW YORK REGIMENT, AT WHITE HOUSE FORD, ON THE POTOMAC RIVER.

and in an appeal to the "fighting stock of the church militant," winds up with this passage: "Much as we have said and done to prove our loyalty, we have not yet resisted unto blood striving against sin. Shall we now, at the call of Christ, come out from behind our velvet-cushioned barracks, whence we have so often hurled bold, indignant words at the giant iniquity of the age, and meet it face to face with the hot shot of rifled artillery, with the gleaming bayonet, or with the clashing sabres in a hand to hand encounter?"

An F. F. V. Outwitted by a Chicago Fire Zouave.—An industrious and shrewd typo from the Queen City of the Lakes, under Colonel Ellsworth, was out on picket duty in the Old Dominion, when a haughty son of the chivalry rode up, driven of course by his "servant." Zoo-zoo stepped into the road, holding his bayonet in such a way as to threaten horse, negro and white man at one charge, and roared out "Tickets." Mr. V. turned up his lip, set down his brows, and by other gestures indicated his contempt for such mud-sills as the soldier before him, ending by handing his pass over to the darkey, and motioning him to get out and show it to Zoo-zoo.

"All right," said the latter, glancing at it, "move on"—accompanying the remark with a jerk at the coat-collar of the colored person, which sent him spinning several paces down the road. "Now, sir, what do you want?" addressing the astonished white man.

White man had by this time recovered his tongue: "What? I want to go on, of course. That was my pass."

"Can't help it," replied Zoo; "it says, pass the bearer, and the bearer of it has already passed. You can't get two men through this picket on one man's pass."

Mr. V. reflected a moment, glanced at the bayonet in front of him, and then called out to his black man to come back. Sambo approached cautiously, but fell back in confusion when the "shooting-stick" was brandished toward his own breast.

"Where's your pass, sirrah?"

"Here, massa," said the chattel, presenting the same one he had received from the gent. in the carriage.

"Won't do," replied the holder of the bayonet. "That passes you to Fairfax. Can't let any one come from Fairfax on that ticket. Move on." A stamp of the foot sent Sambo down the road at a hard gallop.

"Now, sir, if you stay here any longer, I shall take you under arrest to headquarters," he continued.

Mr. V. caught up his reins, wheeled around, and went off at the best trot his horse could manage over the "sacred soil." Whether Sambo ever hunted his master up is not known.

Cross-Examination of some of the "Natives" under Arrest.—A description of the backwoods "we, the sovereign people" of Tennessee, would not be very flattering either to the cleanliness and fashion of their garb, or the quantity or quality of their schooling. The specimens of the masculine gender is invariably adorned in "butternut" pantaloons, without coats, and the feminine in homespun cotton dresses, colored with oak bark and deeply dyed in dirt. It would require but a careless inspection to satisfy one that men, women and children are kept in repair by contractors, and that that class of men are as faithless as in the more civilized and refined regions of loyaldom. When any of these specimens of humanity, for we must class them as such, are arrested, they are taken to headquarters, and submitted to a cross-examination, of which the following may be regarded as a specimen:

General—Where do you live? *Prisoner*—Down thar in the holler.
How long have you lived there? I was born thar.
How long since you left the rebel army? I hain't been thar.
Tell the truth, man. Well I hain't.
Have you no friends there? A cousin, but he was pressed, and wants to get away.
Have you no brothers there? Well there are one, somewhar, but I do'nt know whar.
Are you a Union man? O yes, I was always on your side. All the people here is on your side.
When did you see any of your friends from the rebel army? Not in a long while.
What is the character of the roads around here? Don't know; I never was ten miles from here in my life.
How many men are at Corinth? I don't know; the big folks thar wouldn't tell, if I was to ask them.
Have they a hundred thousand? Don't know how much that is.
Have you any late Southern papers? No; I can't read.
Did the Southern army say anything about the battle of Pittsburg, on their return? They said they's been whipped, and that the Yankees were after them.
Did they retreat to Corinth in order? No; they went helter skelter.
We do not mean to keep you a prisoner only a few days, so that you cannot communicate with your friends. Orderly, take this man away.

Demijohn Drill.—The necessities of the war bring out many laughable, as well as distressing incidents. Whiskey is one of the worst "hangers on" about the National as well as the rebel camps, and is an "artful dodger," hard to rout from the premises. Colonel Marshall, however, of the 8th Maine Regiment lately stationed at Baltimore, has, it seems, invented a penalty against the entering of John Barley-corn into his camp, which promises permanently to expel the intruder.

A correspondent says: "Some one had been permitted to set up a tent inside of our lines, and sell eatables to the soldiers. This individual dared to sell rum, which made a few drunk and noisy. This drunkard-maker was arrested by the Colonel's orders, and taken to the guard-house. His liquor was also seized. He was drummed out to the tune of 'Rogue's March,' presenting a laughable appearance, with a bottle slung over each shoulder, a toddy-stick in his rear, soldiers ahead of him and soldiers behind him with bayonets charged.

After this the sound of shattered glass told us that the demijohn was drilled, and its contents spilled."

In the enemy's lines the reverse seems to be the order of the day, if we may judge from the following: "On the first night after my arrival, in passing from one quarter to another, I was stopped by a sentinel, whom I recognized as private P——, (though he did not recognize me,) I was asked for the countersign and replied, 'A friend with a bottle;' the reply was, 'Advance bottle and draw stopper,' which I did, and was suffered to pass on my way rejoicing." It should be mentioned that private P—— is an Ex-Congressman of Alabama.

Disabling Rebel Guns in Arsenal at Beaufort, S. C.—After the capture of Port Royal, in the early part of November, 1861, an expedition was sent up

DISABLING REBEL GUNS AT ARSENAL, BEAUFORT, S. C.

to Beaufort—the favorite South Carolina watering place—on a reconnoissance. It consisted of the gunboat Seneca, Captain Ammen. Every one remembers that only one white man was found there, and he was drunk. The rebels had evacuated the place, and carried off everything possible. A few guns were left in the arsenal; but as Captain Ammen had no means of taking them away, he disabled them, breaking off the trunnions and burning the carriages.

Coat Worn by Colonel Ellsworth.—The manner and form of this lamented officer's death will be held in remembrance by the people of the United States, and everything connected therewith treasured up as the memento of a truly loyal and courageous soldier. The engraving given above shows the spot where the ball entered the Colonel's breast, and tells how dreadfully accurate was the aim of the assassin Jackson. In other countries such a relic would be preserved with almost national jealousy, proving as it would that defenders of a nation's power is never "forgotten by a free and independent people."

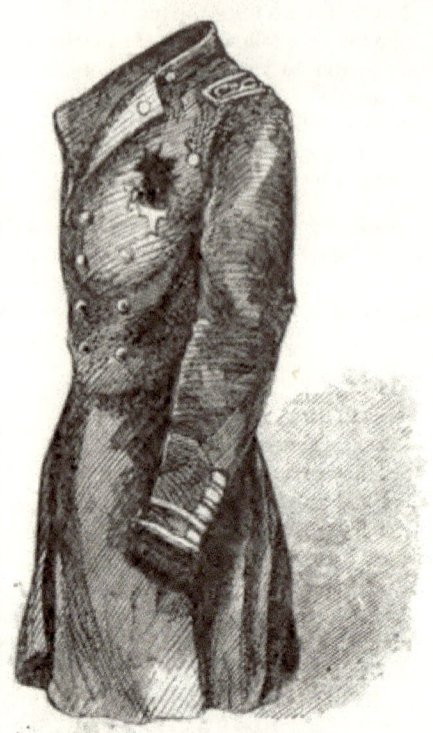

THE COAT WORN BY COLONEL ELLSWORTH WHEN HE RECEIVED HIS DEATH WOUND AT THE HANDS OF THE MURDERER JACKSON.

A Camp of Females at Island No. 10.—We are carried back by the scenes here described, to the times of the Spanish buccaneers, and learn with a blush the abandonment of moral restraint amongst the soldiers of the South.

"On a beautiful hill," writes an officer of Commodore Foote's victorious flotilla, "surrounded by beautiful groves, budding wild flowers, and the accompanying charms of a rural retreat, we found a bevy of nymphs encamped and enjoying soldierly life in real earnest. There were twelve or fifteen of them, of different ages, but all young, and more or less fair to look upon. They sat round the camp fire, and cooked their breakfast, a little disheveled and rumpled, as might, perhaps, be expected, in remembrance of the scenes of excitement they had passed through, but yet as much composed, and as much at home, as though they had campaigned it all their lives. There was a stray lock of hair hanging here and there, an unlaced bodice granting chary glimpses of vast luxuriance of bust, a stocking down at the heel, or a garter with visible downward tendencies—all of which was attributed to our early visit. There were all the marks of femininity about the place. The embowering trees were hung with hoop skirts and flaunting articles which looked in the distance like abbreviated pantaloons. A glance at the interior of their tents showed magnificent disorder. Dimity and calico, silk, feathers, and all the appurtenances of a female boudoir-were visible. It was a *rara avis in terra*—a new bird in the woods.

"These feminine voyageurs were real campaigners. The chivalry of the South, ever solicitous for the sex, could not resist the inclination for its society, and hence the camp of nymphs by the river side, in the embowering shade, *et cetera*. I will not say much for their fair fame, or for the good name of the confederate officers, whose baggage was mingled in admirable confusion with the rumpled dimity and calico, whose boots and spurs hung among the hoop skirts and unmentionables, and whose old hats ornamented the tent-poles or decked the heads of the fair adventuresses. It was a new feature in war."

The Massachusetts 6th in Baltimore.—Sumter has fallen. A call has gone forth for the loyal people to rally to the rescue of the National Capitol, and the defence of the Government and country. Unwarlike in habits and tastes, they nevertheless have come forth from the office, the counting-room, the studio and pulpit, in obedience to their country's summons.

The first in the field were the "Massachusetts 6th." Hurrying from the plow and workshop, they gathered at Lowell, bade farewell to kindred and friends, formed in a solid column, listened with quivering lip to the prayers of their pastor, and the parting addresses of their fellow-townsmen, their bands struck up a national air, their colors were unfurled before them, and the line of march was taken up for Washington.

In seventy-two hours from that time, they were in the heart of Baltimore, and in the midst of an infuriated mob numbering thousands. The particulars of this outrage, and its electric effect on the country at large, are too well known to be repeated here.

It was during the murderous affray of the 19th of April that the following incident took place—an incident fraught with more than usual interest; showing as it did to the world, an example of heroism and daring that deserves the praise of a just and enlightened people.

The regimental band of the Massachusetts 6th, at the time of the attack, consisted of twenty-four pieces, and occupied a separate car. By some mishap this car was "switched off," so that instead of being the first it was left in the rear of the regiment. Thus isolated, unarmed and incapable of making any defence, the members of the band became the objects of attack of the fiendish mob, which immediately commenced breaking up the car with bars of iron, at the same time pouring in a shower of stones through the windows, while others were calling for powder to blow up the car. Finding it would be certain destruction to remain longer thus cooped up, the unarmed musicians leaped out to meet their merciless foe hand to hand. Twenty-four men in a strange city, surrounded by a yelling mob bent on their destruction, while beyond these demons were thousands of citizens silent witnesses of this unequal contest, not daring even to speak a word in behalf of that band of fellow-beings who were seeking in vain for some avenue of escape. Goaded by pain and faint with loss of blood, they were making a final desperate effort to reach some place of shelter, when a rough-looking man sprang in front of their leader, exclaiming—" This way boys! this way!" His was the first friendly voice they had heard since entering Baltimore, and they followed without a moment's hesitation. The strange, rough man led them up a narrow alley to an open door through which they rushed, for their pursuers were close at their heels. Inside they were met by a powerful-looking woman, who grasped each by the hand with the assurance that they were safe beneath her roof.

The last of the band was knocked senseless by a stone as he entered the door, but the amazon who had welcomed them took him up in her arms, and directing his companions to follow, led the way to a room in the upper part of the building, where she immediately commenced to wash and bind up their wounds. After having done this, she procured food for them, and a change of clothes, so that they were enabled to go out in search of their comrades without danger of detection from the ruffianly crowd which had given them so rough a reception. They then learned the particulars of the attack on a portion of their regiment, and of the escape of the greater portion. They saw also the dead and wounded that had been left behind in the hostile city. One of their own number was missing and could not be found, and it was uncertain whether he had been killed or had escaped. On going back to the house where they had been so kindly cared for, they found that their uniforms, together with their battered instruments had been carefully packed up and sent to the depot of the Philadelphia Railroad, where they were advised to go, as they would there be sure to meet friends. They did so, and started in the next train for Philadelphia, and arrived just in time to meet the "Massachusetts 8th" under the command of General Butler, who told them to hurry on to the "Old Bay State," show their battered faces and broken limbs, in the certainty that they would be sent back to play "Hail Columbia" in the very streets of Baltimore, where they had been so inhumanly treated.

The noble-hearted woman who defied a desperate mob in rescuing and protecting those men, is a well-known character in the city of Baltimore. According to the verdict of Christian society she is an outcast, lost to all that is good and elevating; but she is a true heroine nevertheless, and by her noble conduct entitled to the nation's grateful thanks. When Governor Hicks had succumbed to the mob of miscreants, and Winter Davis himself had fled in dismay, and men of influence, of high official standing had hidden themselves in their terror, when all the municipal powers of the city were unable to protect a few unarmed strangers who were struggling for life, then this poor woman, this despised outcast, took them under her protection, dressed their wounds, fed and clothed them, and sent them in safety to their friends.

No doubt thousands of loyal citizens would like to know the name of one who should be remembered for her humanity to their countrymen. It is ANNA MARLEY.

Tobacco Warehouse, Richmond, Va.—This building has recently become somewhat celebrated from its being converted by the rebel authorities at Richmond into a military prison, for the confinement of National prisoners. The tobacco warehouse is situated in the lower part of the city of Richmond, on the south-west corner of Twenty-fifth and Main streets. Previous to its being used as a military prison it was occupied by Messrs. Liggon and Company, for manufacturing and storing tobacco. It is a large three-story brick edifice, built in a substantial manner, and peculiarly adapted for prison and hospital purposes. The main or first floor was allotted to the officers, and the second and third floors to non-commissioned officers and privates. In the centre of the officers' floor was placed the machinery for pressing and preparing tobacco, dividing it into two equal sections—one being used for eating and writing purposes, and the other for promenading and sleeping. The dimensions of this floor are sixty-five feet nine inches by forty-five feet, and the height twelve feet three inches. The room is lighted by five windows on the west or lower side, and three on the east or city side. Those on the east are level with the street, and well protected by iron bars; the west windows are without bars, but were double guarded by sentinels placed in the yard. The window sills on the west side of the building were used as pantries by the stewards, and they often displayed a curious assortment of stores, such as tin cups, plates, knives and forks, a cup of butter, saucer of salt, paper of pepper, loaf of bread, cold beef—comb and brush, whisk broom, towels, a wet shirt drying, shaving apparatus, bottle of vinegar, etc. The room was lighted by gas, the use of which was either

TOBACCO WAREHOUSE, RICHMOND, VA., USED AS A PRISON FOR NATIONAL FORCES.

SCENE AT NEWBERNE—"DRUMMING A COWARD OUT OF CAMP."

kindly or unwittingly given at all hours of the day. It was in this building that the Hon. Mr. Ely was confined, and where he acquired materials for the work which he has published respecting prison life and prison scenes in Richmond.

Drumming a Coward out of Camp.—No matter what may be said, the soldiers of the United States army have evinced in the most unmistakable manner that they were not cowards. They have everywhere, and on every occasion, instead of exhibiting the least symptoms of fear and trepidation, manifested heroism and daring of the highest order. With them the general rule has been a complete recklessness of life. This remark is equally applicable to their conduct and bearing whether under fire or in the more desperate duty of the bayonet charge. To every general rule there is an exception, and it is not surprising that, at such a bloody encounter as took place at Newberne, there should have been a few instances of cowardice. By a wise and salutary regulation of war, the offence of cowardice is deemed one of the gravest which can be committed by a soldier under arms—an offence which renders the offender unfit to associate afterwards with a soldier belonging to the United States army. In the engraving on the preceding page, we have represented in vivid pictorial delineation the coward, after the battle of Newberne, being drummed out of his regiment. The culprit, after having his head shaved, has affixed to his back in large characters the degrading epithet "coward;" the regiment is drawn up, and he passes between the lines, two of his former comrades closely pressing upon him with fixed bayonets, whilst he is preceded by two of the regiment with arms reversed, an indication that the culprit is dead to the corps. He is, in this humiliating position, marched between the ranks. The drummers follow after him, beating the rogue's march. Any one who gives a glance at the illustration cannot fail to perceive the degraded position of the culprit. Certainly such an example must have a permanent and salutary effect upon the minds of men valuing honor and manhood above life.

An Incident of the Williamsburg Battle.—Some years ago, a young Georgian, whom we will for the present call Arthur, came to New York to take a clerkship in one of the leading publishing houses of this city. Of good connection and possessing a fair share of worldly goods, he passed his time pleasantly in the gay metropolis of the Western world. The fearful storm which had for years been gathering in the South, was now casting its deepening shadows on every part of the country; and the roar of Sumter's cannons ushered it in with all its fury. We all remember how New York responded to the duty which this event imposed on her, and how her streets resounded with the tramp of gathering hosts, and the martial music of fife and drum.

Arthur forgetful of his Georgian home, of parents, brothers, and sisters, caught the spirit of the time, and enrolled his name under the "Stars and Stripes," in one of the volunteer regiments of this city. An eventful year passed away, and the army of the Potomac was before Yorktown. The regiment o which Arthur belonged took an active part in the daily conflicts before that position. After its evacuation his regiment was among the advance at Williamsburg driving back the rebels to their stronghold.

The battle of Williamsburg was fought, and we find Arthur among the wounded prisoners who fell into the enemy's hands. He was taken to the common hospital and there left on the bare floor to get along as best he could.

Arthur having obtained some water managed to wash, and dress his own wounds, as well as circumstances would permit. His next object was to escape from the sickening horrors around him, and for this purpose he commenced making his way over and among the dead and dying, which were lying singly and in heaps around him. Among the harrowing sights which met his eye was one, which bound him awe-stricken to the spot. An aged man was kneeling on the rough floor, supporting the lifeless form of a young rebel officer in his arms, murmuring words of prayer, and kissing the pale brow now cold in death. Trembling with conflicting emotions the young Union soldier knelt beside the grief stricken man, murmuring " Father! Brother!"

Arthur has since returned to New York. The story we have told is a true one, as more than one furloughed soldier or denizen of our crowded hospitals can testify.

Nigger-Head *versus* **Grape-Shot.**—During the action that took place off the Forts below the Crescent City on the Mississippi, it is a curious fact that the "contrabands" on board the fleet, suffered very severely. Cannon balls and grapeshot seemed to develop an especial love for them, or that portion of the crew in which they generally served,—the powder division. A fanatical lover of peace might have suggested that it was a judgment upon them, for having been the inadvertent causes of the war. A philanthropical admirer of color might on the other hand have asserted that it was a proof of their courage. A philosophical examiner of cause and effect might impute it to the curious fact that the black is always to be found in the particular place where he ought not to be.

Be this as it may, and to whichever solution of the problem the reader may feel inclined, we shall relate to him an incident which has been vouched for by the correspondent of one of our Journals who was on board the Cayuga.

An individual belonging to the sable portion of mankind and whom we shall take the liberty of denominating Sambo, was employed in passing up powder, on board of the vessel. He was grazed, thrown down and stunned by the force of a spent grapeshot. On coming to, Sambo picked himself up from his recumbent position and felt his forehead, which had been tolerably well bruised by the blow.

"Hi! What's de matter cullud pusson?" inquired the sable cook of the gunboat, as he paused near him on his way to the fore part of the vessel.

"Gol Amighty! dat's de matter," replied Sambo, as he bent over and picked up the two halves of the grapeshot.

"Ay! hi! how?"

"Dat hundert pound—more nor less—hit me 'ere —" ejaculated Sambo, placing his black finger on his then very crimson forehead. "And den de sphrical mass of iron —"

"What? Sambo!"

"Split just into two halves."

"Hi! hi! 'tis n't de fact."

"Den I lie," responded Sambo as he knocked his sable brother down.

Sambo keeps the two halves of the shot as a tangible proof of his assertion. One of the gunners has since this mildly suggested to him, that if he be correct, "nigger-heads would make a capital substitute for round shot." It must be admitted that the thick-skulled darkie has not appeared "to cotton" very warmly to the amiable suggestion.

Planting the Union Flag on Pilot Knob, Miss.—The hoisting of the Union flag in the leading localities captured by the National armies, in their triumphant progress through rebeldom, was at all times hailed with lively satisfaction by the friends of the Union oppressed by the rebel soldiery. At no point did the raising of the Stars and Stripes cause greater satisfaction or exercise a more important influence than at Pilot Knob, Missouri. This State, in the early part of the struggle, gave great cause of uneasiness to the Government, and it became necessary to carry on a vigorous campaign with the view of retaining it to the Union. Many able generals were assigned to this duty; Fremont first took command, afterward Hunter, and then Halleck, aided by such men as Curtis, Siegel, and Mulligan. The task, a difficult and perilous one, was completed—the rebels were hunted "from post to pillar," over the mountains, across the valleys, and in the open plains throughout the length and breadth of Missouri, until refuge was sought amid the mountain fastnesses of Arkansas. During the pursuit of the rebels under Price, the event here illustrated took place. It is one which will not be readily forgotten by the Unionists, whenever they cast their eyes toward "Pilot Knob." This is said to be the highest point in the mountains of Missouri. As soon as the Union army had become masters of that quarter of the State, it was resolved to plant upon its most commanding peak the "good old flag," and send it forth to the breeze that it might herald to all the land that rebellion was suppressed, and that loyal citizens could pursue their usual avocations without let or hindrance, and under the protection of the soldiers who had planted that glorious banner on the wild and elevated summit of "Pilot Knob." The party assigned to this duty was a small one. The illustration shows that they were without implements to dig or raise a mound of earth around their flag-staff. The locality was plentifully supplied with stones and rocks, and with these they built an effectual "cairn," in the centre of which was erected the staff, to which was nailed the honored emblem of the nation.

Graves of the Twenty-Eighth Illinois at Pittsburg.—After the war is over, what pious pilgrimages will be made to sit and linger and weep over the spot consecrated to them who have fought their last battle! The 28th Illinois appropriated an Indian mound near their camp for their own dead, and sur-

PLANTING THE STARS AND STRIPES ON THE SUMMIT OF PILOT KNOB, MISSOURI.

rounded it with a burial fence. The mound is on the highest part of the ground in the vicinity, and is about ten feet above the level, and about eighty feet square on the top. On this the graves are made side by side, in rows, each one having the occupant's name placed at the head, with company and place of residence. It is a sweet spot, surrounded with wild flowers, and when I was last there many of the soldiers were transplanting violets and other wild flowers, to decorate the last resting-place of their brave comrades.

Who was She? An Incident in the Capture of New Orleans. — On April 28th, while the National fleet was anchored off New Orleans, and before the city had been definitely surrendered by the authorities, a small boat, pulled by one pair of oars, was observed leaving the levee. A closely veiled lady was noticed in the stern. When she reached one of the vessels, she drew back her veil and beckoned to the officer of the watch. The Captain, who had remarked that she was young and apparently very lovely, dreaded the influence of the fair syren upon his subordinate, as with a gesture he forbade his responding to the mute appeal, and repaired himself to the gangway. Probably he imagined that forty odd years were more secure than twenty from treasonable temptation.

"Pray, sir," she asked, in the most musical voice imaginable, "might I inquire if a person named McClellan is on board."

At the same time she made him a brief but imperative sign, which he construed to signify that he was expected to reply in the affirmative.

"Certainly there is, madam!"

The white lie may be pardoned on the score of the brilliancy of the flashing eyes which partially bewildered the Captain.

"Might I trouble you to give him this letter?"

As the Captain descended to take it from one of the smallest and most delicately gloved hands he had ever seen, he partially recovered the presence of mind which had not deserted him once during the fierce struggle of the preceding days. He was unwilling that the first pair of bright eyes he had seen for weeks should vanish so quickly.

"Would you not wish to step on board, madam, and speak with him."

A wicked smile flitted over the charming face before him, and but for his age, and the wife he had left in the North, he would infallibly have lost his heart. As it was, he felt it almost going, and laid his heavy hand upon it to check its disposition for levanting from its legitimate owner.

"No; I thank you;" she said. "Such an unexpected pleasure might prove somewhat embarrassing."

Saying this, she again sat down, drew her veil over her face, and making a sign to the colored boatman, was pulled once more towards the levee.

The Captain gazed after her, sighed, and then looked at the letter.

"I suppose I must do duty for McClellan on this occasion," he said. "But who the deuce can she be." He then opened it.

The letter contained a great deal of valuable information respecting the temper of the population of the city. It also stated that Forts Pike and Livingston had been evacuated, and their garrisons despatched to join Beauregard at Corinth, and distinctly affirmed that no Union sentiment could find expression in New Orleans until those who felt it could be guaranteed by the protection of United States troops against the temper of the populace. Subsequent events have proved that the fair correspondent was right; and the young subaltern, who was only able to catch an occasional glimpse of those delightful eyes as she was speaking to his commanding officer, says that, "Never before was the flashing glance of beauty one half so agreeable."

Relative Bravery of Southern and Yankee Troops. — Much gasconade and idle boasting about Southern chivalry and Yankee cowardice may be heard south of Mason and Dixon's line, and a good deal, we are sorry to say, of the same Buncombe obtains with us to the disparagement of Dixie. "Give the devil his due," is applicable here, and besides, what honor is there in a victory over cowards? A conversation that occurred at Fort Donelson between a United States cavalry officers in command, and some distinguished rebel officer who surrendered, comes about as near the truth of the matter as anything we have seen on the subject.

The first rebel officer I met was Lieutenant-Colonel W——, of the 53d Tennessee. He said his arms were stacked, and his regiment ready to be moved off, and asked if I would accept his sword. I passed into his tent, when he handed me his sword. He evidently wanted to say something in the form of speech, but his words choked in his throat, and he could only say: "I would that death had saved me this mortification." Major McC——, of the same regiment, then handed me his sword. The Major was a neat, handsome young man, with light hair, and a complexion as fair as a girl's. He was exceedingly youthful to hold a Major's commission. He said, as he handed me his sword, "I surrender this sword to you, sir, as an evidence of my submission to your superior power; but I do so with deep mortification. I would rather have died in battle." Then two Captains of the same regiment handed me their swords in like manner, and turned their backs to me and wept like children!

I was most deeply touched by this impressive ceremony. I received these acts of submission as graciously as I could. I assured the prisoners of their safety, that they would have humane treatment wherever they might be. I spent at least an hour with these officers. They told all about the fight—how our "sharp-shooters" picked off their men; how our infantry appeared before their entrenchments, as if they had risen out of the ground; how they drove us back, but could not keep us back; and finally, how, wearied with fighting three days and three nights, they became so exhausted that they could hold out no more. They said it was determined on Saturday night to surrender General Floyd announced this determination to all the officers about 2 o'clock, and left soon after. They expressed great indignation that Generals Floyd and Pillow should forsake them, and declared if they had supposed them capable of such meanness, they would never have fought under them.

From this scene I passed rapidly into others, some of a very different character. When I got back to my command, I found one of our Lieutenants had

Colonel Hanson, of the Kentucky 2d, in custody. He was a rough-looking customer, dressed in citizen's dress, short, muscular and blear-eyed—he looked to me as a fit person to command a band of pirates. He said he wanted somebody to tell him where to march his men, that he was tired of waiting. He acted and talked like one having a "heap of authority," and not much like a prisoner. Finding no one to give him immediately the information he desired, he became sociable.

"Well," said he, "you were too 'hefty' for us."

"Yes, but you were well protected by these splendid defences."

"Your troops fought like tigers."

"Do you think now one Southern man can whip five Northern men?"

"Not Western men," he replied, doggedly. "Your troops are better than Yankee troops; fight harder—endure more. The devil and all hell can't stand before such fellows. But we drove them back."

"Why did you not keep us back?"

"You had too many reinforcements."

"But we had no more troops engaged in the field than you had."

"Well, you whipped us, but you have not conquered us. You can never conquer the South."

"We don't wish to conquer the South; but we will restore the stars and stripes to Tennessee, if we have to hang ten thousand such dare devils as you are."

"Never mind, sir, you will never get up to Nashville."

"Then Nashville will surrender before we start."

"Well, the old United States Government is played out—we intend to have a right Government down here."

"What am I to understand by a right Government?"

"A Government based on property, and not a d—d mechanic in it."

"Do these poor fellows all around us here, who have been fighting for you, understand that they are to have no voice in the 'right Government' you seek to establish?"

"They don't care—they have no property to protect."

I thought—confound the fellow—he is the most honest, out-spoken rebel I ever saw. This man is a fair type of the most active, impudent and reckless class of men who have inaugurated this war, to the destruction of every material interest of the country.

Effect of the Gunboat Shells on the Rebels near Port Royal.—The rebel armies during the entire period of hostilities between the North and the South, have been noted for their love of fighting from ambuscades and masked batteries. With these they did serious mischief at Big Bethel, Bull Run, and other points. When the expedition to Port Royal made its appearance there in November, 1862, the enemy, as usual, took to the woods, and practised their military genius upon the loyal forces from their ambuscades. But the naval expedition was under the command of an officer who knew his business, and how to dislodge the enemy, which occasionally became troublesome and

EFFECT OF THE GUNBOAT SHELLS ON THE REBELS IN THE WOODS NEAR PORT ROYAL, JANUARY 1ST, 1862.

at times dangerous. This was done through the medium of shells. When these were fired the chivalrous Southerners never failed to run " helter skelter." Some climbed trees, others squat on mother earth, others again threw away their arms and took to their heels, while not a few fell victims of the destructive missiles, and lost their lives, or were maimed for life, as the penalty of their treason. The accompanying cut represents the bursting of the gunboat shells among the rebels in the woods near Port Royal Ferry, January 1st, 1862, and fully illustrates our remarks. It moreover shows in a véry intelligible manner the destructive and irresistible character of that deadly missile, "the shell." Its passage through the air, its hissing noise, its fall and instant explosion, are alike calculated to appal the stoutest heart.

Mrs. Lincoln on the War.—For the benefit of our lady readers who, with a very natural and laudable curiosity, would like to hear from the lips of the President's wife, her views on the great issue now convulsing the country, we insert part of a letter dated at the White House, June 20, 1861, and which was published in the Louisville *Journal*.

As Mrs. Lincoln has two brothers in the rebel army, one of whom was killed at Fort Donelson, her loyalty has been impeached by her enemies; but this letter at once stamps with falsehood any such malicious imputation.

"Though some years have passed since I left my native State, I have never ceased to contemplate her progress in happiness and prosperity with sentiments of fond and filial pride. In every effort of industrial energy, in every enterprise of honor and valor, my heart has been with her. And I rejoice in the consciousness that, at this time, when the institutions to whose fostering care we owe all that we have of happiness and glory are rudely assailed by ungrateful and parricidal hands, the State of Kentucky, ever true and loyal, furnishes to the insulted flag of the Union a guard of her bravest and best sons. On every field the prowess of Kentuckians has been manifested. In the holy cause of national defence they must be invincible."

We may congratulate ourselves on having so talented and patriotic a lady to preside over the executive mansion.

Economy Taught in War.—It is well to gather a little comfort occasionally, and not brood always on the horrors of war. A Yankee is a peripatetic philosopher under all circumstances, and is apt to "*calculate*" how to make the best of it, wherever he goes. This is one reason why, in the rough and tumble of a campaign, he always has his wits about him, and whilst the lazy rebel is grumbling over his hard fare, he is learning lessons of practical utility for the future. A Massachusetts volunteer, while encamped at Washington, thus wrote in a consolatory letter to his frugal Dorothea:

"I calculate that this war will be an ultimate saving of a handsome fortune to every one who lives to get home, for here we learn that many things heretofore considered as necessities are worse than useless. For instance, the crockery trade will be ruined, and every man will save a handsome sum by substituting tin-ware *ad infinitum*; pies and cake are now seen to be vanity of vanities, and bread and pork to be the only staff of life; and so on through the whole range of domestic economy. My upholsterer is discharged henceforth, and wrapped in my blanket, I lie down to pleasant dreams for the rest of my life."

Marriage amongst the "Contrabands."—About Fortress Monroe are congregated large numbers of negroes who have left their "massa's" plantations for their own and their country's good.

After the day's work, they amuse themselves with dancing, singing, and puffing away at their favorite corn-cob pipes. At the suggestion of a good chaplain, a certain Sunday night was appropriated to joining in the holy bonds of wedlock, such as were disposed to the ordeal. Fourteen couples offered themselves as the happy candidates.

"The room selected for the ceremony was a small one dimly lighted by six candles, suitably placed in position about the room, which shone with a subdued brilliancy upon the ebon faces to the number of about thirty-five males and females, grouped artistically about the clergyman, who was one of the three whites present. The brides were gaily dressed in stunning patterns, and the happy bridegrooms were attired in their best.

"One couple was married at a time, and the sprightly twos that followed came up with a surprising degree of confidence to the parson's call of 'Who's next? Come up.' The ceremony was quickly performed, and the happy couples passed out, leaving an odor of musk floating in the atmosphere, which, in a degree, relieved the air of that closeness which may be observed by attendants on colored churches."

Burying the bodies of Colonel Allen, Surgeon Weller and Second Mate of the A. E. Thompson.—The bodies of these unfortunate soldiers, who met their death by drowning on the 15th of January, 1862, at Hatteras Inlet, were buried under the supervision of Quartermaster Keyes. The only ceremony observed was the lowering of the flag at half-mast on the brig Dragon and a dirge played by the band. The bodies were tightly sewed in canvas, and covered with a coating of tar to exclude the air. They were then deposited in strong boxes, and conveyed to a high sand ridge two miles east of Fort Hatteras, where they were buried, and the spot marked by a wooden slab, bearing their names. Singular to say, there was not any religious ceremony performed upon the occasion. The engraving opposite shows the men in the act of carrying the bodies ashore, and pictures the desolate spot where the mortal remains of these brave men were deposited. The scene is painfully melancholy, and suggests to us the truth of the Scriptural declaration—" In the midst of life we are in death."

Total Wreck of the U. S. Transport New York.—Among the vessels chartered by the United States Government to transport soldiers and munitions of war to Hatteras Inlet, was the screw steamer New York. During the terrific gale which the expedition encountered the New York was driven ashore and became a total wreck. Her cargo—Government stores, was valued at $200,000—

CARRYING THE BODIES OF COLONEL ALLEN, SURGEON WELLER AND THE SECOND MATE TO THEIR GRAVES.

TOTAL WRECK OF THE SCREW STEAMER NEW YORK ON HATTERAS ISLAND, JANUARY 13, 1862.

was all lost. To add to the misfortune the greater part consisted of ammunition, ordnance, etc. The accompanying engraving shows the New York in the gale, with the sea making a clean breach over her.

The Loss of the Pocahontas.—No one whose life has been in any way dependent on the weather, can ever forget the terrible storm of the 13th January, 1862. The sky was covered with clouds of inky blackness, and the sea rode "mountains high." I was one of the crew on board the Steamer Pocahontas on that dreadful night, and, like all my companions, looked with an anxious gaze on the raging elements. It was a night to tax the endurance of the stoutest vessel; and it was to weather such a storm that a wretched old boat, built in 1829, was sent to sea, freighted with a crew of men, and a full deck load of valuable horses.

Surely this was an act most culpable on the part of those who permitted it. Fortunately no lives were lost; but drunkenness and disorder prevailed on board to such an extent that, owing to the wretched management and cruel neglect of their keepers, only 24 horses were saved out of 113.

When the wind rose, and the gale blew about our crazy old boat, a portion of her worthless boiler gave way, and the grates fell down. With considerable difficulty the boiler was plugged or patched up. Then the steering gear gave way. Presently a leak was discovered, and the disorder increased. Instead of attempting in any way to brighten the prospect of affairs, the miserable crew seemed intent on drowning their fears in liquor, with a fair prospect of drown-

LOSS OF THE STEAMER POCAHONTAS, AND DROWNING OF NEARLY 100 HORSES.

ing every one on board in the angry waves that raged around the vessel. To lighten her, magnificent horses, of great value, were constantly thrown overboard. When, at last, the vessel struck, the teamsters who had charge of the poor animals refused to go down on the lower deck and cut the halters of those still remaining there, and they were thus left to perish in the wreck when they might nearly all have been saved. The loud neighing and snorting of the poor brutes, when they found themselves in the water, their mad plunging to release themselves, and their frantic efforts to swim ashore, made a most piteous scene. And as ever and again a fierce, prolonged howl announced the death agony of some poor beast, I shuddered with horror, for nothing is more startlingly touching than the death-cry of a horse. I have heard it when the poor animal was burning to death; and I heard it many a time that night, as one after another, 89 noble horses sunk beneath the dark waters.

I had four companions, all carpenters, like myself, and we all lost every article of clothing and our tools. We were, however, very hospitably received and entertained by the people near Hatteras, where we went ashore, bringing with us the two dozen horses which had struggled through the surf, despite the neglect of their cowardly keepers.

A Brave and Loyal Woman.—An interesting incident is told, concerning the independent and successful stand taken by a woman in New Orleans, in behalf of the Union. She and her husband—a Mississippi steamboat captain—occupied the middle front room of the lowest range of sleeping apartments in the St. Charles Hotel, at the time the city was to be illuminated in honor of secession. She refused to allow the illuminating-candles to be fixed in the windows of her room, and the proprietors remonstrated in vain, she finally ordering them to leave the room, of which she claimed, while its occupant, to have entire control. The rest of the story is thus told:

Determined not to be outdone in a matter of such grave importance, the Captain, who was not in the room during the above proceedings, was next found and appealed to. He heard their case, said his wife had reported him correctly on the Union question, nevertheless he would go with them to the room, and see if the matter could be amicably arranged.

The Captain's disposition to yield was not seconded by his "better half." The proprietors next proposed to vacate the best chamber in her favor, in some other part of the house, if that would be satisfactory; but the lady's "NO" was still as peremptory as ever. Her point was gained, and the St. Charles was doomed to have a dark front chamber.

Pleased with this triumph, Mrs. ——— devised the following manœuvre to make the most of her victory: summoning a servant, she sent him out to procure for her an American flag, which at dusk she suspended from her window. When evening came, the streets, animated by a merry throng, were illuminated, but, alas! the St. Charles was disfigured by its sombre chamber, when suddenly a succession of lamps, suspended on both sides of the flag, revealing the Stars and Stripes were lit up, and the ensign of *the Union* waved from the centre of a hotel illuminated in honor of its overthrow. The effect was to give the impression that the whole house was thus paying homage to the American flag; and what is more significant is the fact that the latter was greeted by the passing crowd with vociferous applause. So much for the firmness of a true Union woman.

How a Rebel Prisoner Attempted to Escape from Fort Lafayette.—A Mr. Lowber, who was arrested for bearing dispatches to the "Confederacy," getting weary of the strong walls of Fort Lafayette, conceived the bold and novel plan of leaving them forever, in a common wash-tub, between one and two o'clock on a dark night in October, 1861. He had procured a key to fit the padlock over the grating of the port-hole of his casemate, also a rope and a life-preserver. Some coin and his gold watch he packed in a bladder and put in his pocket, and placed his valise in the tub. He then fastened the rope to the tub, let the tub out of the port-hole, and, after securing the rope, bid goodbye to Fort Lafayette, and entered the tub himself. He set sail for the land, all the time watched by the sentinel, who allowed Mr. Lowber, his tub and its cargo to land on the dock in safety. But no sooner had he landed than he was commanded to surrender or be shot. Of course, Mr. Lowber did not like the shooting proposition, so he surrendered, and suggested to the sentinel that he might take the bladder containing the gold watch and the $47.50 in money, and allow him to go back into the fort through the port-hole, and have nothing said about it. But the sentinel would not consent. He alarmed the garrison, and Lieutenant Wood, the officer of the post, had the prisoners' roll called to see if all his guests were in the fort. He then had Lowber secured in double irons, and placed in the guard-house.

Lowber said that he had not succeeded, but that if he had, by that time (afternoon) he would have been in Dixie's land. He told the officers in charge that they might look for a better rebel, but they would have to go further south than Fort Lafayette to find a truer one.

It appears that Mr. Lowber has recently received some visits from ladies with skirts of an extraordinary size.

Clearing the Battle-field after an Engagement.—Few can form an adequate idea of the horrifying and repulsive aspect of a hotly contested battle-field the day after the fight. The accompanying representation shows the Union soldiers burning the dead horses, near the Peach Orchard, after the battle of Pittsburg Landing. As will be observed, the ground is literally strewed with the slain animals, the decay of which, would be apt, in popular language "to breed a pestilence" among the troops in their neighborhood. To prevent this, burning the dead animals is an easier as well as safer practice than burying them.

"Clearing the battle-field" however means more than the mere disposing of the poor dead brutes that man has pressed into service. It means the gathering of the wounded, the burying of the slain, and the removal from the face of the fair earth and the eye of heaven, of the hideous traces of man's rage and wickedness. This sad task can only be described by those who have partici-

CLEARING THE BATTLE FIELD—BURNING THE DEAD HORSES NEAR THE PEACH ORCHARD.

pated in it, and over its horrors the impulses of humanity bid us draw a veil. The pencil tells the story all too vividly to the eye.

Capturing the Rebel Steamer Darlington in Fernandina Harbor.—The United States expedition which visited Florida in the month of March, 1862, had, for the most part, an easy and a bloodless victory at every point on the sea coast where it touched. Invariably, as soon as the Union gunboats made their appearance the rebel forts were evacuated, their garrisons flying to points of safety in the interior. Fernandina was no exception to the rule, although pretty capable of making a strong resistance.

Fort Clinch and its other defences were abandoned, and the inhabitants of the city left to make such terms as they might be able with the Union commander. While retreating from Fernandina, the rebels embarking on a railway train which was to carry them beyond the reach of the naval expedition, had the temerity to fire upon one of the gunboats; this was responded to by a shell while they were in the woods near the railway bridge. The bridge, it appears, crosses a river through which steamers and sailing craft often pass. In consequence of the bridge being closed to allow the train to carry off the runaway rebel soldiers, one of the steamers plying between Jacksonville and Fernandina, was brought to a stand. She was observed by one of the gunboats, and from having the rebel ensign insultingly floating at her mast head.

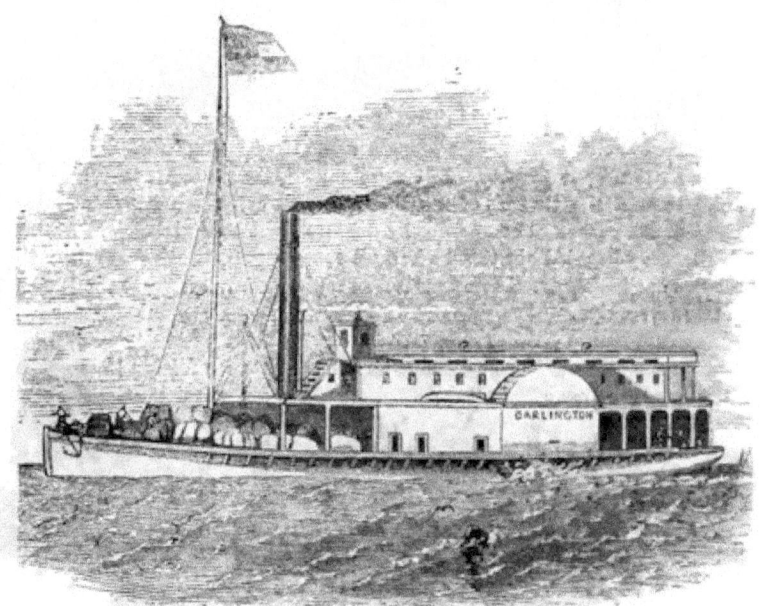

REBEL STEAMER DARLINGTON, CAPTURED IN FERNANDINA HARBOR.

was at first taken for a rebel gunboat. Captain Rodgers ordered her capture, and as there were no means of escape she fell an easy and undisputed prey to the officer and men sent after her. As will be perceived from the engraving, she was only a coasting steamer; she had, however, in addition to a cargo of provisions, a large quantity of the baggage and other effects of affrighted citizens, who undertook to escape into the interior as soon as the Union fleet entered their waters. It is related that when the Darlington was captured the terror of the passengers on board, was beyond all description; they fancied there was nothing before them but an instantaneous death. In vain did the Union officers and men declare their peaceful and humane intentions and repudiate any thought of interfering with their persons or their property—all was in vain. The rebel chiefs had thoroughly instilled distrust and hatred of the Union forces into their hearts. At length these misguided people, most of them females, were induced to listen to reason, and finally to acknowledge that no matter who might come to rule over them, they could not be worse off, nor treated with less consideration than they had been whilst under the control of the rebel mob which had so ingloriously abandoned them upon the first approach of danger.

Naval Heroism.—Not only have our officers of the National Fleet distinguished themselves, but the Jack Tars at the guns, have in several instances, if possible, outrivaled their superiors in undaunted coolness and indifference to physical pain. What can be more sublime in suffering than the enthusiastic and unflinching devotion of this brave blue-jacket to his post! Let him, if he still lives, be promoted, and receive a vote of thanks, too, from Congress, though he be but an ordinary sailor.

During the progress of the engagement at Port Royal, a shot fired by the enemy entered one of the legs of a seaman named Thompson, while he was at the helm, shattering it terribly. Nothing daunted, the wounded man, seizing his knife, severed the tendons of the limb, and, throwing the member away, remained at his post until compelled by debility to be carried below. As he was borne away he cried out that he had set the compass, as calmly as though his life was not in danger. Thompson is now rapidly convalescing at the Naval Hospital in Brooklyn.

A Serious Joke.—Mr. Secretary of State Seward, between foreign imbroglios and traitors at home, has had a perplexing and unpleasant post. Though fond of wit, a *bon-mot*, or anything provocative of humor and a good hearty laugh, he is not to be trifled with in matters affecting the dignity and diplomacy of his country, as will be seen from the subjoined anecdote.

A representative of one of the five Great Powers met Mr. Seward one day just as he was coming out of his office on his way to dinner. Of course, the diplomat was invited to walk in. He declined, saying, "Oh no, I only called to tell you a good joke. One of our captains has just arrived, and says that when he reached Charleston, and went to our consul's office, and inquired for the consul, he was told that he was drilling his company. What company?

inquired the captain of the ship. Why, one of the companies selected to march against Washington. The captain was greatly surprised, and mentioned the fact as evidence of the universal feeling of hostility which pervades Charleston."

Mr. Seward.—What is the name of your consul at Charleston?

Diplomat.—His name is B——.

Mr. Seward.—(Opening the door opposite where they were standing.) Mr. Assistant Secretary, draw up an order *recalling* the *exequatur* issued in favor of Mr. B——, Consul at Charleston. There, that business is disposed of.

Diplomat.—My God, Seward! You are not in earnest. I only told you the story as a good joke.

Mr. Seward.—And I, my Lord, avail myself of this "joke" to give you practical evidence of the manner in which we intend to deal with every foreign power and its representatives, whenever they interfere, directly or indirectly, between us and the traitors in rebellion against our Government.

The Old Flag.—New Orleans, the Empire City of the South, which Old England with a picked army couldn't take, fell before the valor of New England, and the heroic Butler presides over the crest-fallen metropolis of the Creoles.

A National flag that had seen service, was displayed in Boston in honor of the capture of New Orleans. It bears the following inscription: "This flag was banished from New Orleans when Louisiana voted to secede. It will be used there again to celebrate the glorious victories of the Union."

"Two years ago it was first used in New Orleans at the inauguration of the the statue of Henry Clay. In January, 1861, when the city was illuminated to celebrate the secession of Louisiana, it served the purpose of a carpet, to prevent injury from the burning candles. After several months' service in the Union cause, it now waves to celebrate the victory at New Orleans, and in a few days will be returned to that city in triumph, to be re-established in its original position."

Infernal Machines.—Traitors are generally cowards, and cowards are devilish in their animosities and brutal in success. The truth of this is verified by the diabolical devices of the rebels as exemplified in the engraving annexed. When the United States flotilla was about to ascend the Potomac, the rebels conceived the idea of blowing up the Pawnee and the other vessels composing the expedition. For this purpose they set adrift a number of "Infernal Machines" in the river, where the Pawnee and her consorts were lying. By means of the machine it was hoped to blow up the squadron. The following is a description of the machine represented in the engraving. Two large eighty-gallon oil casks, perfectly water-tight, acting as buoys, were connected by twenty-five fathoms of three and a half inch rope, buoyed with large squares of cork every two feet, secured to casks by iron handles. A heavy bomb of boiler iron, fitted with a brass tap, and filled with powder, was suspended to the casks six feet under water. On the top of the cask is a wooden box, with fuse in a gutta-percha tube. In the centre of the cork was a platform with a length of fuse coiled away.

INFERNAL MACHINE DESIGNED BY THE REBELS TO DESTROY THE UNITED STATES FLOTILLA IN THE POTOMAC.

occupying the middle of the cask. It was intended by the contrivers of this weapon of civilised warfare that the shock of a collision should light the fuse.

Testimonial to the Hero of Fort Sumter.—How the heart warms up and the pulse quickens at the name of General Robert Anderson! Who does not recollect the hopes and fears which agitated every Northern bosom, when the first gun boomed against that fortress, where for two days imprisoned within its fast-falling walls, the brave commander and his little garrison defied a host of assailants. And not until his quarters were burned, and the red-hot shot and shells were falling thick and fast through the breaches, and there was danger every moment of an explosion from the unprotected magazine, did the undaunted Anderson consent, hopeless and helpless, to lower the glorious banner of the Stars and Stripes.

Then started, as from a sleep, the aroused spirit of an infuriated people; then rolled the drum in every city and village, on every mountain and in every valley throughout the land; then, from the workshop and the farm-house, the counting-room and the factory, mustered and swarmed the hundreds of thousands of armed avengers, who are now sweeping like a hurricane through the South, and will soon again, over that very fort, unfurl that same "old flag!"

General Anderson, on his release, was welcomed with the shouts of thousands wherever he moved. The freedom of cities, swords, crowns of laurel, and every demonstration of sympathy and admiration were tendered him. Amongst the most beautiful, was a gold medal presented on the 10th of July, 1861, by the Mayor of New York, on behalf of its citizens, as a recognition of his courage and fortitude at Fort Sumter, and in appreciation of his character. The medal is of solid gold, three inches in diameter, and of the intrinsic value of $500. The word "Sumter" surmounts the representation of an extensive fortress in mid-ocean. Shells are exploding over its parapets, while shot is flying from the guns on the ramparts, and flames are bursting from the embrasures. On the reverse are the thirty-four stars blended in a wreath of oak leaves, with this inscription: "PRESENTED TO MAJOR ROBERT ANDERSON BY THE CITIZENS OF NEW YORK, AS A SLIGHT TRIBUTE TO HIS PATRIOTISM." The mottoes, "*Pudens, Fidelis et Audax,*" and "*Invictæ Fidelitatis Præmium,*" form the sentiment.

Coolness of Melancthon Smith.—One of the bravest of our brave in the action which resulted in the passage of the Forts by our fleet, and the capture of New Orleans, would appear to have been Melancthon Smith, then in command of the *Mississippi*. It was this officer who with his vessel destroyed the rebel ram *Manassas*. Always known to be a man of courage we hardly think his best friends would have suspected how great an amount of pluck and daring lay concealed under his quiet exterior. As his vessel, in obedience to the orders of Commodore Farragut, was passing up the river, which if not her actual progenitive, had given her its name, and in doing so, was in what to a nervous man must have appeared a very unpleasant propinquity to Fort Jackson, he occupied himself in pacing up and down the hurricane deck leisurely, in the thickest of the iron hail-storm, the enemy were pouring around her. His orders had all been given. The men were engaged in obeying them or looking after their guns. There was at the moment nothing more pressing for his attention than the need of a little mild exercise for the benefit of his constitution. But his mind was restless. He felt that it required some soothing mechanical employment. What could be better for him at such a juncture than a full-flavored Havana. A naval commander who objects to the weed, might be preserved after death in a national museum as an unrivalled philosophical and natural curiosity. And so Melancthon Smith passed his hand into the breast-pocket of his coat, extracted his case, opened it and very carefully selected a cigar. Having passed it between his lips, he then looked around to see where he might procure a light.

His First Lieutenant alone was to be seen upon the deck with him. He appeared to be watching as much of the enemy's operations on the other side of the thick walls of the Fort, as he could obtain a glimpse of through the casemates when the smoke gave him a chance of seeing them. To tell the truth, this could scarcely have been much.

"The deuce!" his commander muttered to himself. "I suppose I must hail below for one."

At this moment his sharp eyes detected a cabin boy possessed of more curiosity than courage, peering out on the fort from behind some cover.

"Here, you young skulker!" he sung out in tones that were distinctly audible through the roar of mortar and cannon. "Run below, and get me a light."

The First Lieutenant looked round and then stepped towards him.

"What is it?" inquired Melancthon Smith.

"Nothing particular, Sir!" replied the officer, who was very nearly as cool as himself—"but I believe you wanted a match, and I happened to have one about me."

"Ha! indeed! Thank you. You are very kind," responded his superior, taking it from him. "And now, might I ask you to stand before the wind that I may have a chance of lighting it."

So saying he occupied himself for a moment in scraping it against the deck and lighting his cigar. A ball from the fort passed close to them as he threw the match away.

"By the bye!" said Melancthon Smith as if half apologetically, "don't you think it would be quite as well to keep at a little distance. Those scamps," he added, "are not the best marksmen in the world. They may however manage to hit a double mark. A single one, they are pretty sure to miss."

The Lieutenant could not avoid smiling, as he heard this. However, with a bow, he gave his assent to the philosophy of his commanding officer, and crossed to the other side of the deck. It strikes us that it would be well nigh impossible for coolness in danger, to exceed the superb *sang-froid* displayed by his commander.

It is told of the same officer that when the *Mississippi* was drawing near the forts with the purpose of passing them, his men commissioned a deputation to wait upon him.

"Well! my lads!" he inquired, "What is it?"

"Why! your honor!" answered the spokesman of the party, touching his forelock in an awkward attempt to display his respect, "the boys are very dry."

"Did I not order them a ration of coffee, half an hour since?"

"Yes! your honor!" was the reply of the speaker. "But —"

"But, what?"

"The boys were thinking they'd like to splice the main-brace, purvided you've no objection."

"No, no! my lads! d—n it, we'll have no Dutch courage. When our work is done, all who have not gone to glory, shall have their liquor."

He was too well known by his men for them to dream of attempting to change his decision. So, they went into action that day without their grog. When it was over, however, they had it served out to them liberally, for Melancthon Smith has never been known by them to break a promise that has been given, or to forget his word when it has once been passed.

Gathering the Wounded in Blankets after the Battle of Pittsburg Landing.—All who have read the detailed accounts of the battle at Pittsburg Landing are aware that the slaughter on both sides was terrific, and that the rebels fought on that occasion with more than their accustomed bravery and determination. The sketch on the next page faintly pictures the scenes which were witnessed after the two bloody engagements had terminated,—the removal of the dying and wounded soldiers. Poor fellows! so fearfully maimed were many of them that they were unable to move, others were shattered and bruised by repeated wounds that they could not bear to be borne away in the arms or on the backs of their comrades and fellow soldiers. The only means left was to place them in blankets supported by four men, one at each corner. In this easy position they were carried to the nearest point where they could obtain surgical relief and hospital accommodation. Upon glancing at the illustration one does not know which to admire most, the heroic bravery of the sufferers, who although in actual torture and severe bodily pain, seem calm and resigned, or the delicacy and tenderness evinced by the soldiers appointed to bring the wounded off the battle-field. By the side of the wounded men, who are being carried off the field, lie the mortal remains of a horse and its rider. Both have been slain, and until all the wounded are removed, they must lie uncovered by mother earth, a feast for vultures and beasts of prey. It is in contemplating pictorial illustrations like these that we are led to exclaim "Oh war, how terrible art thou in all thy aspects! Death, destruction and evil in every shape and form, are thy constant attendants! The jubilant shout of victory is stifled by the moans of the wounded, and the groans of the dying. Thy mission is more Satanic than Godlike, for at all times and on all occasions injustice, deceit and despotism, are the ruling motives of those who send forth to the world the preliminary plea, a declaration of hostilities!"

A Safer Berth during Sub-marine Operations.—Science when applied to war does not always ensure the safety of those who employ it. Although

HEROIC INCIDENTS AND ANECDOTES

BATTLE OF PITTSBURG LANDING—GATHERING THE WOUNDED IN BLANKETS AFTER THE BATTLE

OF THE CIVIL WAR IN AMERICA. 85

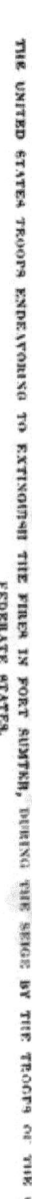

THE UNITED STATES TROOPS ENDEAVORING TO EXTINGUISH THE FIRES IN FORT SUMTER, DURING THE SIEGE BY THE TROOPS OF THE CONFEDERATE STATES.

no one in the incident we are about to relate received any harm, it may be considered a very fair proof of the preceding axiom. Mr. Julius Krahl, the well-known sub-marine operator, was employed in our navy at the mouth of the Mississippi. When the vessels arrived off the forts, and we believe before the bombardment began, he went out with Captain Porter and others of the officers of the expedition in boats to experiment on the wreck of a sunken raft. The charge which he employed was some thirty pounds of powder, and when he had arranged it, the boats retired to what they considered a tolerably safe distance. When the torpedo was fired however, its explosive force was terrific. It tore the huge logs apart as if they had been so much paper, scattering their heavy fragments through the air in all directions. A large number of these fell around and beyond the boat in which Captain Porter and Krahl were sitting.

"Good God!" exclaimed the latter, as he ducked his head to avoid a fragment which fell unpleasantly near them, "what a narrow escape we have had."

Porter had not moved.

He, however, smiled grimly, as the middy in charge of the boat looked round and observed, "Don't you think Mr. Krahl, the next time a closer berth to the object might be somewhat safer."

Scene at the Bombardment of Fort Sumter.—The long-threatened overt act of the rebellion, was the bombardment of Fort Sumter, in Charleston harbor, South Carolina, on the 13th of April, 1861. The rebel batteries plied with fearful rapidity and exactness upon the doomed fortification. Major, now General Robert Anderson, replied with much vigor and determination to the fire of his assailants until the rebel batteries had set the barracks on fire. The accompanying illustration was sketched at the time the United States troops were endeavoring to extinguish the flames. When the rebels saw the smoke rising above the fortification as from a hell, with loud shouts they redoubled their fire, as if to leave no element of atrocity wanting in their impious attack on the majesty of the nation. The scene in the fort at this time is thus described by one of the garrison.

"We had eaten our last biscuit thirty-six hours before. We were nearly stifled by the dense smoke. The men lay prostrate on the ground with wet handkerchiefs over their mouths and eyes, gasping for breath. If an eddy of wind had not ensued, we should all have been suffocated. The crashing of shot the bursting of shells, and the roar of the flames made a Pandemonium of the fort. We nevertheless kept up a steady fire."

How our Sailors Fight.—But a faint idea can be formed of the gallantry and endurance displayed by the crews of our gun and mortar boats in the battle off the forts below the Crescent City, by those who only read the accounts given of it in the daily journals. Even the pictorial paper, far as it outstrips general journalism by the varied resources which it brings to bear upon such a subject, is unable to represent one half of the bravery and horror of such a struggle. It may illustrate the grandeur and terror of the scene, but it fails to individualize the suffering and endurance. These can only be indicated by the pen or the pencil.

As an instance of what we mean, we may mention that when the last shot from the guns of the *Varuna* was fired, her decks were under water. The sailors stood bravely to their work, while those of their fellows who had been wounded, were drowning beneath their very feet. The imperious call of duty forbade their flinching. None thought of his own or his fellow's safety while it was possible to do anything on behalf of the flag of their country. When the ship finally settled in the water, nothing was saved beyond their scanty fighting trim. Not a stitch of clothing save that—not the daguerrotype of this one's darling, which was carried in his jacket pocket—not the Bible given that one by his dead mother—not the lock of hair from the head of Ethan's wife—not the love-letter Isaac had last received, had been left them. So long as they had felt a plank under their feet, they had done their duty to that starry banner under the shadow of whose broad folds their God had first called them into life.

Escape of two Union Soldiers on a Raft.—Among the Union prisoners captured at Bull Run were James McRorty and Peter Kelly of the 69th New York Militia. Being allowed to go out in Richmond to make purchases, they bought a couple of dark grey hunting shirts, such as were worn by the Virginia troops. In this disguise, on the 18th of September, they passed the sentries in broad daylight, in company with Sergeant O'Donahue and other prisoners, and gained the outskirts of Richmond, travelling all night and resting in the woods all day. After many narrow escapes and many long and weary journeys, these loyal adventurers succeeded in reaching a hill overlooking Aquia Creek. They carefully avoided going near the habitations of the people for fear of being detected, and the only human being they met was an occasional negro returning from a corn-husking spree. The only food which they brought from Richmond was two pounds of crackers, this lasted them for two days. The rest of the time they subsisted on the ears of green corn which they roasted in the woods. Just as they succeeded in getting a view of the Potomac, they narrowly escaped a rebel cavalry picket, which was out on scout. They skirted the shore cautiously, working towards Occoquan Creek, where they concealed themselves for three days in a fish house, watching the chance of escape to the United States squadron, which they saw on the Potomac. This was a period of cruel suspense and suffering, but still they were lucky enough to pick up an old cooking pot, which enabled them to boil their corn. About this time they observed a sloop stranded on shore, and as no better chance was likely to offer, they set about constructing a raft, which, however, was not sufficient to carry off the whole party. Sergeant O'Donahue embarked alone on it, and was picked up and taken by the Seminole to Washington. The other two men, McRorty and Kelly, finding that O'Donahue had only thought of his own escape, and that he did not send a boat for them, embarked on another raft which they had constructed. The engraving on the opposite page represents these brave fellows in the act of crossing the Potomac. One is acting as oarsman, propelling the raft, whilst the other is signalizing the

88   HEROIC INCIDENTS AND ANECDOTES

ESCAPE OF TWO UNION SOLDIERS ON A RAFT.

the Penguin, war steamer, which bears down to their relief. They were put on board the steamer Yankee on the 30th of September, at 4 o'clock A. M., and from her transferred to the Reliance, which carried them to Washington, where they received all the aid and comfort which their worn-out condition so much demanded.

Rebel Commissioners and London Capitalist.—Money is not only necessary to furnish the sinews of war, but the financial credit of a nation is generally a test of its ability to command respect and assistance in time of trouble. Hence the failure of the South to obtain loans abroad, although many there pretended to sympathize with them in their insurrectionary organization.

An interview between some of their prominent agents and the great house of Baring Brothers, shows the opinion entertained of their honesty and solvency in the metropolis of England, and is thus described by a gentleman present.

They commenced with a most elaborate and glowing description of the resources and wealth of the Rebel States. After a pause:—*Mr. Bates.* Have you finished? *Commissioners.* Not quite. [Then a speech from Commissioner No. 2, and a pause.] *Mr. Bates.* Have you finished? *Commissioners.* Almost. [Then a speech from Commissioner No. 3, and a pause.] *Mr. Bates.* Are you through? *Commissioners.* Yes, sir; you have our case. *Mr. Bates.* What States did you say composed your Confederacy? *Commissioners.* Mississippi, South Carolina, Alabama, Georgia, Florida, Texas, and Louisiana. *Mr. Bates.* And Mr. Jefferson Davis is your President? *Commissioners.* He is. We are proud of him. *Mr. Bates.* We know Mr. Davis well by reputation. He is the same gentleman who stumped his State for two years in favor of Repudiation, and justified the conduct of Mississippi in the United States Senate. We know the gentleman; and although we have no reason to be proud of him or his antecedents, I think I may safely say, that if you have brought with you to London the necessary funds to pay off principal and interest, the repudiated millions owing to our people by your States of Alabama, Mississippi, and Florida, there is a reasonable prospect of your raising a small amount in this market! Our Mr. Sturgis will be happy to dine you at 8 o'clock to-morrow evening! *Exeunt omnes.*

While this scene was being enacted at the Baring's Mr. Dudley Mann waited upon our countryman Peabody, who holds $300,000 of Repudiated Mississippi Bonds, on which there is due more than $60,000 of interest. Mr. Mann was very magnificent and grandiloquent, but withal, prosy; and Peabody, suffering from gout and Mississippi Repudiation, lost his temper; and shaking his clenched fist at the rebel, emphatically said: "If I were to go on 'Change and hunt up the suffering and starved widows and orphans who have been ruined by your infamous repudiation of honest debts, and proclaim that you are here to borrow more of our gold and silver to be again paid by repudiation, (as I believe it is my duty to do,) you would inevitably be mobbed, and find it difficult to escape with your life. Good morning, sir."

Poor Fellow!—Some of the calamities attendant on the rebellion are enough to melt a heart of stone, even though the victim be an enemy. Amongst the wounded prisoners in the camp hospital at Shiloh, one poor, emaciated Southerner was sitting upon a large chair, with a couple of Union surgeons attempting to staunch the blood which had been pouring from a terrible hole in his side. He evidently was dying, and after his wound was dressed he asked for Mr. Barclay, who went and sat down beside him. The man said he could not last much longer, and he wanted Mr. Barclay to promise to have him buried, so that his mother could get his body when the war is over. The promise was given, a prayer was read, and after saying that he could not be treated more kindly at home, and that he only wished his people could know how good those of the North were towards the sick and wounded of the South, he felt more composed, and fell asleep. To-day his bed is empty.

A Sad Result.—Of the living martyrs in the South, made so by being outspoken friends of the Union, the case of one in Norfolk is perhaps as pitiable as any in the long catalogue. A year ago he was worth $30,000, every dollar of which the rebel government confiscated. He took to the woods and swamps south of Norfolk; and upon hearing that the old flag waved once more over his native city, he returned. Meeting an old Northern friend on the streets, he threw himself into his arms, and fell to the ground a shrieking maniac. The convulsion of joy was too much for mind and body, enfeebled by his starving life in the woods, and he is now a lunatic.

Reward for Courage.—Pensions for our brave soldiers, medals, and bounty lands are all very proper, but one of the most inspiring incentives to deeds of noble daring, and one which can be seen at all times in its honorable resting-place, is a general order issued by Colonel Paine, of the 4th Wisconsin regiment. It commands that the Government colors of the regiment shall be placed, at the close of the war, one in the Senate Chamber and the other in the Assembly Chamber at Madison, Wisconsin, and that within one month after every battle in which the regiment shall be engaged, the surviving officer highest in rank shall cause a careful examination to be made into the conduct of all the members of the regiment, of every class and rank, and shall cause the names of the five most distinguished for heroic behavior on the battle field, together with the names and date of the battle, to be embroidered in gold within a wreath of gold, on each of the regimental colors. The name of the highest surviving officer may be included in the five, upon the written recommendation of nine-tenths of the survivors of the battle.

"Poor Dog Tray, Ever Faithful."—The attachment of the canine friend of man is deep, and remains even after death has robbed him of his master. If Byron wrote an epitaph on sculptured marble over his pet Newfoundland, the dog without a name, in our story, deserves at least to have his fidelity chronicled in our records of the war. The wife of Lieutenant Pfieff went on the mournful errand of finding the body of her husband who was killed at the battle of Pittsburg Landing. "No person, when she arrived on the field, could inform her where her husband's corpse was buried; and after searching among the thousands of graves for half a day, she was about to abandon the pursuit in despair. Suddenly she saw a large dog coming toward her, which she recognized as one which had left Chicago with her husband. The dog seemed delighted to find her, and led her to a distant part of the field, where he stopped before a single grave. She caused it to be opened, and found the body of her husband. It appears by the statement of the soldiers, that the dog was by the side of the Lieutenant when he fell, and remained with him after he was buried. He then took his station by the grave, and there he had remained for twelve days, until relieved by the arrival of his mistress, only leaving his post long enough each day to procure food."

Secession Currency not a Legal Tender for Drinks.—The citizens of the once flourishing "Dixie," have brought on their own heads and pockets, by their silly attempt at an independent government, nearly all "the ills that flesh is heir to." Their ports are blockaded, and all commerce stopped, and the petty business they do, in a retail way, in the larger towns is represented by a sham imitation currency, "rags and shinplasters." As an illustration of their value, the following laughable affair came off at the Mills House, Charleston. One of the aforesaid shinplasters read thus, "The council of the city of Charleston certify that this may pass for 5 cents." Two of them being offered for a "tod," the barkeeper handed them back saying, "'tods' paid in that way are 30 cents, or 10 cents each in the coin of the 'old concern.'"

Secretary Walker's Plantation.—Little did this notorious gentleman, who forms one of Jeff. Davis' Cabinet, and who boasted on the fall of Fort Sumter that his rebel flag should in less than six months wave over the dome of the Capitol at Washington and the venerable roof of Fanuiel Hall, think that in one short year the Federal army would be marching over his magnificent estate, and his abandoned houses and negroes be wholly at its mercy.

Shortly after entering Alabama, we passed his vast plantations, extending along the road for miles. The mansion was utterly deserted and the furniture removed. A perfect host of negroes came down to see and to welcome us. They laughed, they sang, they danced in their glee. I stopped a moment to converse with them. "By golly," said a fine-looking, honest young negro, "I'se a great notion to go along with dis crowd! what do you say, Massa?" "My poor friend," I replied, "if you did, you will probably be turned out of our lines at the first place we encamp; somebody who claims you will come and take you back; and then, besides being severely punished for running away, you will in every respect be worse off than before." The negro understood me. "It is very hard, Massa," said he. His voice faltered; I saw that tears were gathering in his eyes, and I rode away, as my own were growing moist and dim.

A detached house upon General Walker's plantation was enveloped in flames when I passed. It had been set on fire by some of our soldiers, but whether accidentally or not, I did not stop to enquire. One of the negroes had a heavy iron ring and a bolt fastened to his leg. He said he had worn them for more than three months. A cavalryman descended quietly from his horse, knocked off the fetters, fastened them to his saddle, and rode away. "By heaven," I heard him mutter, "I would forfeit a year's pay for the privilege of transferring these to the leg of the rascal who put them on that man."

Headquarters of General Pope at New Madrid, Island No. 10.—The gallant conduct and bearing of this accomplished general and soldier have endeared him to the people of the United States, consequently every thing connected with his movements, in the war to put down the rebellion, will be treasured up with care. The humble dwelling which he occupied during the seige at that important stronghold, Island No. 10, therefore, becomes invested with interest.

The last Shot from the Cumberland.—The daring exploit of the iron-clad war steamer Merrimac has created a greater revolution in the art of war than any previous incident of the last three or four centuries. Until checkmated by the United States floating battery Monitor, the Merrimac dealt destruction to every thing which came in her way. Two of the United States ships of war—the "Congress" and the "Cumberland"—succumbed before her invulnerability and superior power. The "Congress" was run ashore, crippled, and obliged to surrender. The "Cumberland" shared a still worse fate; but she was defiant to the last. A gunner, who had both his legs shot away, strode up to his gun on his bloody stumps, drew the lanyard, and with a shout for "the old flag," fell back, dead. And as the vessel went down, her gallant tars fired her bow gun, the only one remaining above the water, in defiance, at the exultant enemy. A moment later and the Cumberland disappeared, her top mast, with her battle flag flying, alone remaining above the surface of the bay.

HEADQUARTERS OF GENERAL POPE AT NEW MADRID, DURING THE SIEGE OF ISLAND NO. 10.

THE FIGHT BETWEEN THE MERRIMAC AND CUMBERLAND—LAST SHOT FROM THE SINKING CUMBERLAND.

One of the crew of the Cumberland, James Marlaw, who was on board when she went down, but escaped by swimming, tells us: "The shot of the Congress and Cumberland had no more effect upon the Merrimac than if they had been as many peas or apples. We had no other alternative but to stand and fight like men. When the Captain of the Merrimac called on Lieutenant Morris to surrender, the latter shouted back, 'Never!' Then," continues the sailor, "he backed his infernal machine off again, and the Cumberland fired as rapidly as she could, but the Merrimac again ran her steel prow into her side. Again Lieutenant Morris was summoned to surrender the ship, and back again went the reply, 'Never!'"

CLOSE not this page of History yet,
 Nor let unfilled the record stand,
For never must the world forget
 How sunk the brave ship Cumberland.

Not in the cold and thoughtless night,
 Of sad oblivion and loss,
Can she come shattered from that fight,
 Without the Crown, to bear the Cross.

Lift her where coming time shall see,
 And sound her name to years remote,
While yet the banner of the Free
 In glory o'er the waves shall float!

How, while her life ran out, she fought,
 Sing to the Future; for the Past
No memory has, not e'en in thought,
 Of such a fight, to death at last.

Through weary hours she strove—for what?
 Ah! little deemed she Victory's wreath
Should crown her brows: she hoped it not,
 But wrought to reach a glorious death.

Full fast the waters drifted in,
 And still was heard her cannon's boom;

Though Fortune would not let her win,
 She could not fill a craven tomb.

When through her ports the cruel waves
 Poured fiercely down upon each gun,
Still, ere they found their watery graves,
 The men discharged them one by one.

And at each roar their wild huzzas
 Rang loudly on the salt sea air;
They hailed aloud the Stripes and Stars
 That still defiant floated there.

At last one gun alone remained,
 The waters gurgle round her. "Fire!"
The noble ship, her crest unstained,
 Sought 'neath the waves a new empire.

An empire in the hearts of men,
 An estate in a nation's praise;
A glorious life in death, and then—
 A monument for after days.

O God! if there be honors yet
 For those who die to aid the Right,
Let not thy mercy, Lord, forget
 The men who fought that glorious fight.

A "Special Correspondent" in the Discharge of his Duties.—We who read the papers, and these, we flatter ourselves, interesting pages, know but little and think less of the pains and penalties inflicted on the poor and much-abused scribes, who furnish us the romance of the war whilst suffering themselves its realities. As a specimen we give the following graphic sketch of an unfortunate "special" seeking a night's rest:

We had been in the saddle since four o'clock in the morning, some of us had run down our horses carrying orders, until they were actually unable to bear us longer, and we were still more exhausted than the horses. Where the General was we couldn't find out, and so we resolved to lie down, right where we stood, and trust to chances for not getting between both fires in case of a rebel sortie. Luckily the rebel regiment had retired in too big a hurry to take all its blankets, and Captain Mallory, who was in charge of them, was able to furnish us a couple of thin ones. With these we lay on the ground, and in an instant were sleeping. Presently some one shook us up, and succeeded in getting us to comprehend that in case of a night attack, we might find it convenient to leave that point without having to spend time in saddling and bridling our horses. Altogether it was thought safest to attend to that matter at once, and so at it we went, groping about for the saddles, getting the wrong bridles on the wrong horses, and vice versa, till in some shape we tied up the persecuted animals again, sank down on the ground, and in a moment were asleep.

How long we slept I don't know—I don't suppose anybody does—but I do know that it seemed but an instant, and a very unsatisfactory instant at that. A sentry who was watching the captured property stirred us up with the cheering information that we were some distance outside the lines, and in the very skirt of the woods through which the enemy was expected to attack. With the profound skepticism that sleepy-headedness can best produce, we utterly scouted the possibility of an attack, and insisted, with much sleepy logic, on our right to sleep where we pleased, enemy or no enemy. But the sentry wouldn't listen to reason, and so we had to get up. Leading our tired horses after us, we began a dreary stumbling walk among the hills to find the General's headquarters. We might as well have hunted through those fields for the seraglio of the Grand Sultan.

Noticing a two-wheeled concern, with a horse tied to each wheel, but none to the shafts, we hailed the omen, opened the door, and tried to crawl in, when we suddenly came in vigorous contact with the heels of a brace of sleepers who had preceded us, and "pre-empted" the narrow territory. We tried another ambulance. It contained a little straw and three men, one of them alone weighing 250. Back we groped to our two-wheel bobtail, crawled under, certain that the horses at the wheels couldn't tramp on our heads, and profoundly indifferent as to what they might do to our legs. It began to rain, but who cared? Our heads were under the ambulance, and what more need anybody want? And so we went to sleep once more.

Pretty soon there was a commotion among the ambulances, horses, drivers, and squatters. The General was out there roaring. "Take away all this stuff; what are you doing right before our lines where you would be riddled by the first fire from either side? Away with you at once."

Determined this time to get where we wouldn't be pestered any more by somebody's telling us that we were between the opposing lines, we begged the General to tell us where we could lie down in quiet. "Do you see that log stable over yonder?" "Yes, Sir." "Well, that's a hospital; get behind that." Off we went, stole some hay for our horses, spread our rebel blankets in the fence-corner, and lay down.

In the morning, I found that the hard place in the ground I had complained of, was a tremendous Spanish stiff-bit bridle, on which I had rested more soundly than I ever did on a hair mattress. After so much selection we had finally slept on a fragrant manure pile!

Knowing that we might have to spring to our saddles in a moment, we had not removed our spurs, and true to the instincts newspaper men are popularly supposed to possess, each had been diligently raking his spurs up and down the legs of the other! Who says we didn't sleep soundly when at last we got at it?

They had hurried us off the morning before from Muddlethy bottoms without our breakfast, reconnoissance had taken the place of dinner, and trying to find somewhere to rest our weary heads that of supper. The wagons had still not come up, and not a mouthful of food did I get on that morning of the second day, till about 11 o'clock I shared with General Rosecrans, in Floyd's tent, some biscuits baked at Floyd's stove from secession flour. It's all very pleasant to write about now, but if anybody thinks the duty of an army correspondent an easy one, let him try it.

Execution of an Alleged Spy.—After trial at Richmond, by a court-martial, of Timothy Webster, as an alien enemy, on the charge of lurking about the armies and fortifications of the Confederate States of America, the prisoner was found guilty.

On the 29th of April last, under escort of the Provost-Marshal, he was led to the execution. Before starting, he asked the clergyman to read the Psalm of David, invoking vengeance on his enemies. He refused, and Webster grew indignant, causing the clergyman to take an early departure. When brought to the gallows, the prisoner was visibly affected by the sight of the preparations observable, and shuddered when he looked at his coffin. After the rope was adjusted around his neck, prayer was offered up by the Rev. M. D. Hoge.

At the conclusion, a black cap was drawn over his eyes, he having previously bid farewell to several persons standing by. The signal being given, the trigger struck against the uprights with a loud sound. Owing to the defective cotton rope, the noose slipped, and Webster fell on his back to the ground. The half-hung and partially stunned man was speedily raised and assisted up, and a new rope being ready, he was soon swinging in accordance with his sentence. This occurred at 11.22 o'clock. Fifteen minutes later we left the ground, but the body was still suspended. He died in about one minute.

Webster, who had plenty of gold and C. S. Treasury notes, gave it all to his wife the night before his execution. He was in the employment of one of the departments here as a letter-carrier between this city and Maryland. It is said —how true we know not—that he used to take the letters received here to Washington, where they were copied, and the answers received served in the same way, thus being used as evidence against the parties, as many of them have found to their cost by subsequent arrest and incarceration in Northern forts.

Iron Plated Gunboat New Era, on the Missouri River.—The "New Era" is one of the gunboats which was stationed on the Missouri river for the purpose of maintaining the supremacy of the United States Government in those waters. It is entirely plated with thick boiler iron, and carries 10 Dahlgren guns and a crew of 100 men. The lower part of the New Era is con-

IRON PLATED STEAM GUNBOAT NEW ERA, ON THE MISSOURI RIVER, CARRYING TEN DAHLGREN GUNS.

structed of heavy 10-inch oak timber, well seasoned. Upon an examination of the accompanying engraving, it will be perceived that the principle developed in Charleston harbor—that of placing the iron facings at an angle so as to glance off shot—has been partially adopted in the defences of this vessel. During the Missouri campaigns, the New Era performed much useful and important service.

Skedaddle.—This word, like demoralize, and some others, has become stereotyped for the war. Some scholar has found out its root, and traces it to the Greek language. At all events, it is so popularized as to have inspired some genius to immortalize it in song. As a general rule, parodies are simply detestable, but this is really so good and funny, that Longfellow himself, should he meet with it, will pardon the profanation of his sublime "Excelsior."

The shades of night were falling fast,
As through a Southern village passed
A youth who bore, not over nice,
A banner with the gay device,
 Skedaddle!

His hair was red; his toes beneath
Peeped, like an acorn from its sheath,
While with a frightened voice he sung
A burden strange to Yankee tongue,
 Skedaddle!

He saw no household fire, where he
Might warm his tod or hominy;
Beyond, the Cordilleras shone;
And from his lips escaped a groan,
 Skedaddle!

"Oh, stay," a cullered pusson said,
"An' ou dis busson res' your hed!"
The Octoroon she winked her eye,
But still he answered with a sigh,
 Skedaddle!

"Beware McClellan, Buell, Banks,
Beware of Halleck's deadly ranks!"
This was the planter's last Good Night,
The chap replied, far out of sight,
 Skedaddle!

At break of day, as several boys
From Maine, New York, and Illinois,
Were moving southward, in the air
They heard these accents of despair,
 Skedaddle!

A chap was found, and at his side
A bottle, showing how he died,
Still grasping in his hand of ice,
That banner with the strange device,
 Skedaddle!

There in the twilight, thick and gray,
Considerably "played out" he lay:
And through the vapor, dun and thick,
A voice fell, like a rocket stick,
 Skedaddle!

Perilous Aerial Voyage of General Fitz-John Porter over Yorktown.—Amid the many hair-breadth escapes of our gallant officers, none, both from its novelty and danger, is more thrilling than that of General Fitz-John Porter. It was necessary to have a reconnoissance of the enemy, and Professor Lowe's balloon was selected for the bird's-eye view.

He supposed the usual number of ropes were attached to it, whereas there was only one, and a place in this, as was afterwards ascertained, had been burned by vitriol, used in generating gas. Taking his seat in the car, unaccompanied by any one, the rope was let out to nearly its full lenghth—the length is about nine hundred yards—when suddenly snap went the cord, and up went the balloon. This was an unexpected part of the programme.

Quickly a squad of cavalry, led by Captain Locke, Lieutenant McQuade, of the General's staff, plunged spurs into their horses and dashed away in the direction of the descending balloon. The rest of the story is, as I have received it from the General's own lips. While the rope was being payed out, he adjusted his glass in readiness for his proposed view of the enemy's territory. A sudden bound of the balloon told him the rope had given way. He saw the wind had taken him over the line of rebel intrenchments. Having no wish to drop in among them, he left the valve to take care of itself, and proceeded to take advantage of his position to note the aspect of rebel objects below. Crowds of soldiers rushed from the woods, and he heard their shouts distinctly. Luckily he was above the reach of their bullets, so he was not afraid on this score. The map of the country was distinctly discernable. He saw Yorktown and its works, York River and its windings, and Norfolk and its smoking chimneys. A counter current of air struck the balloon, and its course was reversed. Its retreat from over rebeldom was rapid. He opened the valve, the gas escaped and down he came. He could not say how fast he came down, but it was with a rapidity he would not care to have repeated. The car struck the top of a shelter tent, under which, luckily, no one happened to be at the time, knocked the tent flat, and left him enveloped in a mass of collapsed oil silk. He crawled out, and found himself in the middle of a camp, not one hundred rods from General McClellan's headquarters.

Upper Story of House Occupied by Gen. Wright near Fort Walker.—. The prefixed engraving shows the house which General Wright occupied near Fort Walker (Port Royal). The design of the sketch is to illustrate the effects of a shell which, entering the upper portion of the house, burst in the room, carrying away the partitions on that floor, and destroying the greater part of the furniture. This instance is another of the many proofs extant that shells are the most dangerous and destructive of missiles.

Take your Choice, Madam.—At Nashville, the ladies have been peculiarly spiteful and bitter against the hated rival which waves victorious over the stars and bars. It sometimes happens, however, that they are compelled to render a formal obedience at least to the spangled folds.

Over the large gate at the Provost Marshal's splendid headquarters—Elliott's female school—waves a Union flag. A very ardent secesh lady, who wished to see Colonel Matthews, was about to pass through the gate, when looking up she beheld the proud flag flapping like an eagle's wing over his eyrie. Starting back horror struck, she held up her hands and exclaimed to the guard:

"Dear me! I can't go under that dreadful Lincoln flag. Is there no other way for me to enter?"

"Yes, madam," promptly replied the soldier, and turning to his comrade, he said:

"Here, orderly, bring out that rebel flag and lay it on the ground at the little gate, and let this lady walk over it!"

The lady looked bewildered, and after hesitating a moment, concluded to bow her head to the invincible Goddess of Liberty, whose immaculate shrine is the "Star Spangled Banner." The rebels may all just as well conclude to follow her example.

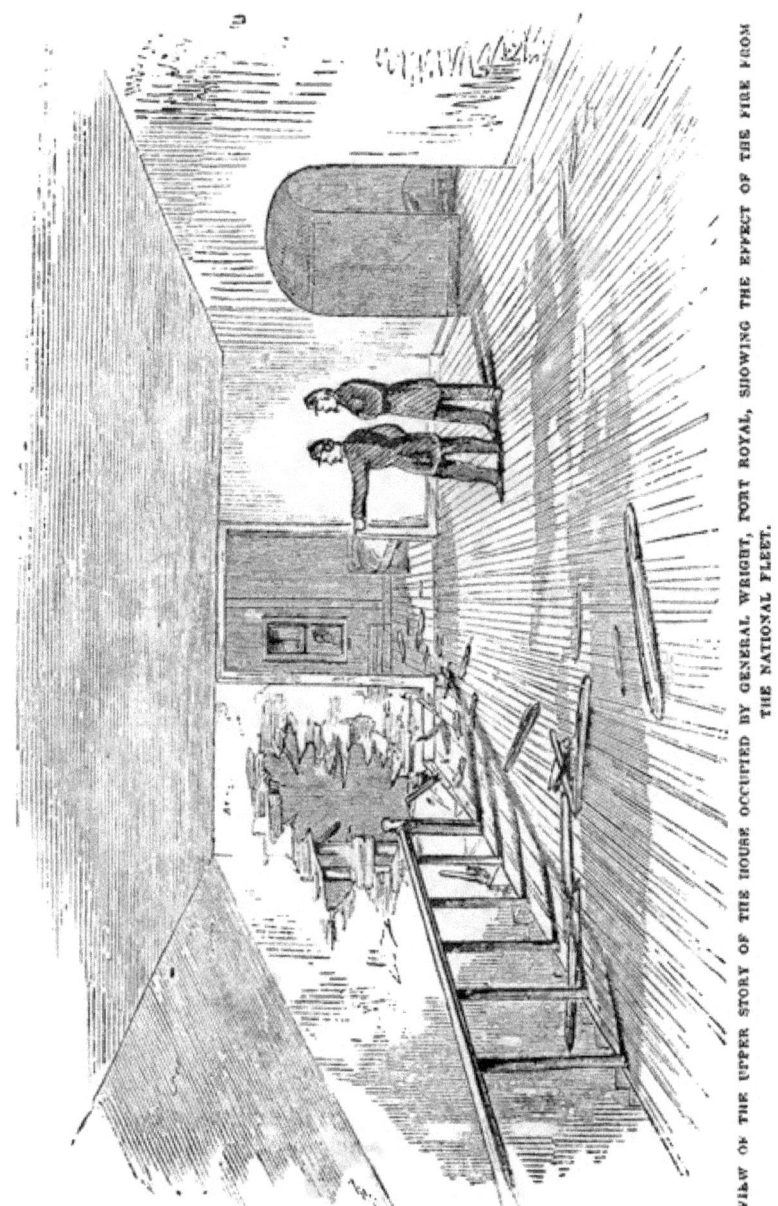

VIEW OF THE UPPER STORY OF THE HOUSE OCCUPIED BY GENERAL WRIGHT, PORT ROYAL, SHOWING THE EFFECT OF THE FIRE FROM THE NATIONAL FLEET.

www.ingramcontent.com/pod-product-compliance
Lightning Source LLC
Chambersburg PA
CBHW031119160426
43192CB00008B/1041